VMware NSX Network Essentials

Learn how to virtualize your network and discover the full potential of a Software Defined Data Center. A smarter way to use network resources begins here

Sreejith.C

BIRMINGHAM - MUMBAI

VMware NSX Network Essentials

First published: September 2016

Production reference: 1220916

Published by Packt Publishing Ltd.
Livery Place
35 Livery Street
Birmingham
B3 2PB, UK.
ISBN 978-1-78217-293-2

www.packtpub.com www.packtpub.com

Credits

Author
Sreejith.C

Copy Editor
Safis Editing

Reviewer
Deepal Verma

Project Coordinator
Judie Jose

Acquisition Editor
Vinay Argekar

Proofreader
Safis Editing

Content Development Editor
Amrita Noronha

Indexer
Aishwarya Gangawane

Technical Editor
Deepti Tuscano

Graphics
Disha Haria

Production Coordinator
Nilesh Mohite

Foreword

Credits

Over the past few decades, we witnessed how virtualization changed the landscape of a modern data center. It revolutionized how an under-utilized server hardware could be effectively utilized and in turn secure the ROI for businesses. In fact, virtualization is the first step towards helping organizations realize the goal of Software-Defined Data Center (SDDC). Now it's time for networks to go through the similar drift and step into new world of SDDC, with the advent of Network Virtualization(NV) and Software-Defined Networking (SDN). Although network virtualization and SDN appear to be the same from an end output perspective, there are subtle nuances between the key functions they both offer to traditional networks. While network virtualization provides a way to create an abstraction layer on the underlying physical layer to create networks, SDN concentrates on consolidating the control plane for these networks. VMware NSX leverages both the network virtualization and SDN concepts to provide a feature-rich networking and security platform for its customers. NSX is a big leap towards achieving VMware's vision of SDDC. With NSX for vSphere in place, customers can seamlessly extend virtualization to network and security services and also bundle them with automation capabilities.

There has been a lot spoken and written lately about VMware NSX in the networking industry over the past few years. If we take a step back and look at where all this started, we quickly come across a company called Nicira, which arguably introduced the SDN concept to the industry back in the 2000s. In 2012 when VMware acquired Nicira, a new transformation started for virtual networks which enabled them to offer networking and security functionality that is typically handled in hardware directly in hypervisors. In short, NSX successfully enabled customers to abstract, reproduce, and automate the traditional network and security services in software.

I don't want to spill the beans just yet in this foreword. I would let you explore all the awesomeness of NSX by yourself in the upcoming chapters of this book. This book provides you good foundations on Network Virtualization and SDN along with how NSX uses them both to provide network services to SDDC. You will be shown the detailed step-by-step instructions to install and configure NSX. In addition, you will also be learning how to leverage NSX to implement logical switching, routing (both static and dynamic), edge services gateway, distributed firewall, VPN configurations, data security, and so on.

Hope you are going to like it, and happy learning!

Pavan Kumar Thota

Staff Technical Training specialist

About the Author

Sreejith.C is a solution consultant at the Mannai corporation based out of Qatar. He specializes in storage, virtualization, private, public, hybrid cloud, and SDN. He determines customer requirements and designs VMware Cloud-based solution architectures spanning VMware's product portfolio from the vCloud Suite to meet the functional and business requirements of various sizes of organisation, and across verticals. He holds various advanced and professional certifications: VCAP-CIA,VCAP 55-DCV,CCNA-DC, VCP-NV, VCP-CLOUD-5/6, VCP- 6/5/4, EMC-ISA, EMCISA-V2, EMCIE, and MCTS-AD2008. He has instructed multiple candidates on EMC and VMware technologies on a wide range of products such as Symmetrix, VMAX, vCloud Director, VCNS, NSX, and vCloud Air. He enjoys speaking at customer forums by sharing his ideas and also participates in VMware Community forums. You can contact him on LinkedIn ID at `http://www.linkedin.com/pub/sreejith-c/44/b3/a2a`

Sreejith is married to Sthuthi and they are blessed with a beautiful daughter called Naomi.

I would like to dedicate this book to my family, who have immensely helped in my career, and last but not least, my colleagues with whom I have worked so far in VMware and Wipro Technologies.

About the Reviewer

Deepal Verma is a senior systems engineer who specializes in virtualization and storage technologies. He has worked in a variety of technical roles for over 10 years and holds industry certifications including VMware Certified Implementation Expert - Network Virtualization (VCIX-NV), VMware Certified Professional 6 – Network Virtualization (VCP6-NV), VMware Certified Professional 6 – Data Center Virtualization (VCP6-DCV), VMware Certified Professional 5 – Data Center Virtualization (VCP5-DCV), and others from AWS, EMC, and NetApp. His passion is to continue to learn new technologies and make it easier for others to understand. Deepal has also been recognized as a VMware vExpert (2016) for his contributions to the VMware community.

www.PacktPub.com

For support files and downloads related to your book, please visit `www.PacktPub.com`.

Did you know that Packt offers eBook versions of every book published, with PDF and ePub files available? You can upgrade to the eBook version at `www.PacktPub.com` and as a print book customer, you are entitled to a discount on the eBook copy. Get in touch with us at `service@packtpub.com` for more details.

At `www.PacktPub.com`, you can also read a collection of free technical articles, sign up for a range of free newsletters and receive exclusive discounts and offers on Packt books and eBooks.

`https://www.packtpub.com/mapt`

Get the most in-demand software skills with Mapt. Mapt gives you full access to all Packt books and video courses, as well as industry-leading tools to help you plan your personal development and advance your career.

Why subscribe?

- Fully searchable across every book published by Packt
- Copy and paste, print, and bookmark content
- On demand and accessible via a web browser

Table of Contents

Preface

NSX has transformed data center networking by introducing security and automation in Software Defined Data Centers (SDDC) . Software-defined networking is highly dynamic and helps organizations scale their data centers. By making use of the feature-rich services in VMware NSX, organizations can improve their CAPEX and OPEX. This book provides a comprehensive coverage of various software-defined networking features offered by VMware NSX.

What this book covers

Chapter 1, *Introduction to Network Virtualization*, this chapter starts with evolution of virtualization and introduction to software defined data center followed by Network Virtualization discussion. We will also be covering how network virtualization has changed traditional datacenter networking by discussing various uses cases and features of VMware NSX.

Chapter 2, *NSX Architecture*, understanding NSX architecture is key for knowing features and various use case of NSX. Here we will be primarily covering Management Plane, Control Plane & data plane architecture followed by VXLAN architecture which will be essential for understanding the creation of Logical networks and troubleshooting virtual networks during upcoming modules

Chapter 3, *NSX Manager Installation and Configuration*, we start this chapter with all requirements needed for a successful NSX installation by following step by step instruction on deploying and configuring NSX manager, NSX Controller and Data Plane software modules for Logical Switching, routing and Microsegmentation.

Chapter 4, *NSX Virtual Networks and Logical Router*, with the fundamental understanding on Overlay network in the previous chapters here we will be discussing about Logical Switching and distributed logical routing. Starting from configuration we cover step by step instructions on how to deploy Logical switches and establish a simple routing environment within the hypervisor layer.

Chapter 5, *NSX Edge Services*, we start this chapter with introduction to NSX Edge Services and various form factors. We also have discussions around NAT, DHCP, Load balancing and routing in this chapter and with that knowledge this chapter will be a complete network package that NSX offers in Software defined datacenter.

Chapter 6, *NSX Security Features*, end to end security is key to the success of any network topology. We start this chapter with introduction to traditional way of securing networks and how NSX helps to have a better control within Virtual Space. Distributed Firewall, Service Composer are some of the key highlight's of this chapter

Chapter 7, *NSX Cross vCenter*, one of the most exciting feature of NSX is Cross vCenter Server. Ability to manage multiple vSphere Environment and leverage NSX features is a game changer in modern day datacenter. In this chapter we will have a deep dive sessions on Architecture and deployment of NSX Cross vCenter with some design backing the topology discussed in the chapter.

Chapter 8, *NSX Troubleshooting*, this chapter is all about applying what we learnt so far to identify and resolve NSX installation, registration and log process steps. The chapter is written in the same order how we started with the architecture of NSX – Management Plane, Control Plane and Data Plane troubleshooting followed by upgrade scenarios.

What you need for this book

Primarily,we need NSX Manager,vCenter Server and ESXI Hosts with Local/remote storage.

Note that for an NSX Manager to participate in a cross-vCenter NSX deployment the following conditions are required.

Above configurations can be configured and tested even on a Nested ESXI environment ,however it is strongly not recommended to deploy it like that in a Production Environment.

For hardware compbatility matrix, please do refer VMware HCL guide: http://www.vmware.com/resources/compatibility/search.php

Who this book is for

If you're a network administrator and want a simple but powerful solution to your network virtualization headaches, look no further than this fast-paced, practical guide.

Conventions

In this book, you will find a number of text styles that distinguish between different kinds of information. Here are some examples of these styles and an explanation of their meaning.

Code words in text, database table names, folder names, filenames, file extensions, pathnames, dummy URLs, user input, and Twitter handles are shown as follows: "All it does would be a traditional broadcast, `ff:ff:ff:ff:ff:ff` (destination MAC)."

Any command-line input or output is written as follows:

```
net-vdr --route -l default+edge-19
```

New terms and **important words** are shown in bold. Words that you see on the screen, for example, in menus or dialog boxes, appear in the text like this: "From NSX Manager, navigate to manage **IP Pools** and click on the + sign."

Warnings or important notes appear in a box like this.

Tips and tricks appear like this.

Reader feedback

Feedback from our readers is always welcome. Let us know what you think about this book-what you liked or disliked. Reader feedback is important for us as it helps us develop titles that you will really get the most out of. To send us general feedback, simply e-mail `feedback@packtpub.com`, and mention the book's title in the subject of your message. If there is a topic that you have expertise in and you are interested in either writing or contributing to a book, see our author guide at `www.packtpub.com/authors`.

Customer support

Now that you are the proud owner of a Packt book, we have a number of things to help you to get the most from your purchase.

Downloading the color images of this book

We also provide you with a PDF file that has color images of the screenshots/diagrams used in this book. The color images will help you better understand the changes in the output. You can download this file from `http://www.packtpub.com/sites/default/files/downloads/VMwareNSXNetworkEssential s_ColorImages.pdf`.

Errata

Although we have taken every care to ensure the accuracy of our content, mistakes do happen. If you find a mistake in one of our books-maybe a mistake in the text or the code-we would be grateful if you could report this to us. By doing so, you can save other readers from frustration and help us improve subsequent versions of this book. If you find any errata, please report them by visiting `http://www.packtpub.com/submit-errata`, selecting your book, clicking on the **Errata Submission Form** link, and entering the details of your errata. Once your errata are verified, your submission will be accepted and the errata will be uploaded to our website or added to any list of existing errata under the Errata section of that title.

To view the previously submitted errata, go to `https://www.packtpub.com/books/conten t/support` and enter the name of the book in the search field. The required information will appear under the **Errata** section.

Piracy

Piracy of copyrighted material on the Internet is an ongoing problem across all media. At Packt, we take the protection of our copyright and licenses very seriously. If you come across any illegal copies of our works in any form on the Internet, please provide us with the location address or website name immediately so that we can pursue a remedy.

Please contact us at `copyright@packtpub.com` with a link to the suspected pirated material.

We appreciate your help in protecting our authors and our ability to bring you valuable content.

Questions

If you have a problem with any aspect of this book, you can contact us at `questions@packtpub.com`, and we will do our best to address the problem.

1
Introduction to Network Virtualization

Starting from the mainframe days, server virtualization has a long history. However, today's data centers use virtualization features to abstract physical hardware, which would be a pool of resources such as CPU, storage, and memory, to the end users in the form of virtual machines. The easiest way to ensure server resource utilization is improved is through virtualization techniques. Server virtualization success has been hailed as a transformational event in data centers primarily because a single physical machine can run multiple operating systems and each operating system can be managed like a dedicated physical machine. This is a very simple but highly powerful solution. There are different types of virtualization, such as server, storage, application, desktop, and the industry's newest buzzword is network virtualization. Network virtualization has been on the market for a long time. VLANs, VPNs, MPLS, VPLS, and VSS are all widely used examples of network virtualization. If you have worked in a data center, you would agree that networking is always challenging to work with. Network architects are forced to perform manual configuration, which results in configuring VLANs, ACLs, routing, firewall rules, QoS, load balancing, and so on. The drawback for this model is complex and slow, and in a dynamic cloud environment, the complexity would increase.

In this chapter, we will cover the following topics:

- The traditional network model
- The three pillars of a **Software Defined Data Center** (SDDC)
- Introducing the NSX-V network virtualization platform
- The power of server virtualization and network virtualization
- How to leverage NSX
- VMware NSX features

The traditional network model

Traditional architecture was built on a classic three-tier hierarchy. Each of these layers will have one or more network devices for redundancy and availability reasons:

- **Data Center Core Layer**: The core layer is the backbone layer, which offers faster delivery of packets by getting interconnected to multiple aggregation layer devices that provide high-speed switching. It is best not to configure any traffic-filtering features at this layer.
- **Aggregation Layer**: The aggregation layer is a mediator between the core and access layers. It is best to configure routing and filtering polices at this layer.
- **Access Layer**: The access layer is ideally where end user machines are directly connected either to the **top of rack (ToR)** switch or at the **end of row (EoR)** based on the network design.

The following screenshot is an example of a classic three-tier network architecture:

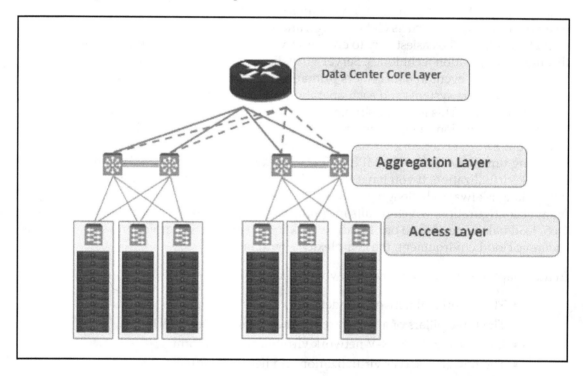

Let us now ask ourselves the following few questions:

- How can my network, storage and server team work together if there is a performance bottleneck?
- How many VLANs, STPs, LACPs, and routing configurations are required?
- Will a change in application requirement demand a change in physical network?
- Do I need to repeat initial configurations such as Vlans, STP, LACP, and routing?
- Are all my features dependent on hardware devices?
- Is isolation of tenants/virtual machines tied to VLANS?
- Do I need to re-architect my applications before they can work with public cloud?
- Does migrating, (VMotion) a VM from server-server will demand a change in physical network configuration?
- Do I have end-to-end network visibility from a single pane of glass?
- Where is firewalling taking place, outside the rack or inside the rack?

The preceding Q&A list is long and, yes, networking is stuck in the past and there is only one solution—*It's time to virtualize the network!*

The three pillars of a Software Defined Data Center

In a **SDDC**, all elements of infrastructure, that is storage, networking, and compute are fully virtualized and delivered as a service. It is described by VMware as *"A unified data center platform that provides unprecedented automation, flexibility, and efficiency to transform the way IT is delivered. Compute, storage, networking, security, and availability services are pooled, aggregated, and delivered as software, and managed by intelligent, policy-driven software"*. An SDDC is the mechanism through which cloud services can be delivered most efficiently. One of the key goals of an SDDC is to build a cloud-based data center. Vendors such as Amazon, Google, IBM, and VMware all have their own set of public cloud services running on an SDDC stack . Yes, now we have a next-generation data center wherein we could pool all physical servers and let applications run according to IT-defined policies.

As the heading suggests, the three pillars of SDDC are shown in the following screenshot:

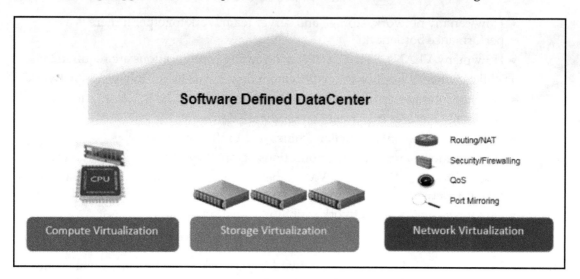

Let's go through each of them one by one:

- In **Compute virtualization,** CPU and memory are decoupled from physical hardware and each application resides in a software object called a virtual machine. VMware VSphere, Microsoft Hyper-V, Citrix XenServer, Oracle VM are a few examples in that family.

- **Storage virtualization** in a **Software Defined Storage** (**SDS**) environment is a hypervisor-based storage abstraction from the heterogeneous model of physical servers. Software that enables an SDS provides most of the traditional storage array features, such as replication, deduplication, thin provisioning, and snapshots. Since this is a completely software-defined storage, we have increased flexibility, ease of management, and cost efficiency. In this way, pooled storage resources can be automatically and efficiently mapped to application needs in a software-defined data center environment. VMware VSAN is a classic example of SDS since it is a distributed layer of software that runs natively as a part of an ESXi hypervisor.

- **Network virtualization** is the third and most critical pillar of a **Software Defined Data Center** (**SSDC**) center and gives the full set of Layer 2-Layer 7 networking services such as routing, switching, firewall, load balancing, and QoS at the software layer. Network virtualization is the virtualization of network resources using software and networking hardware that enables faster provisioning and deployment of networking resources. The innovation speed of software is much faster than hardware and the answer for the future is not a hardware-defined data center but a Software Defined Data Center which will let us extend the virtualization layer across physical data centers. What makes Amazon and Google the world's largest data center is the brilliance of Software Defined Data Center. Network virtualization provides a strong foundation by effectively resolving all traditional network challenges to ensure we are getting a fully-fledged SDDC stack. As the cloud consumption model is being rapidly adopted across the industry, the need for on-demand provisioning of compute, storage, and networking resources is greater than ever. Network virtualization decouples the networking and security features from physical hardware and allows us to replicate similar network topology in a logical network.

Introducing the NSX-V network virtualization platform

Since we have defined what network virtualization is all about, let's discuss VMware NSX and its history. **Nicira** (**NSX**) was a company which focused on software-defined networking and network virtualization and was founded by Martin Casado, Nic Mckeown, and Scott Shenker in 2007. On July 23, 2012, VMware acquired Nicira and NSX is a product which was created from VMware **vCloud Networking Security** (**vCNS**) and the Nicira network virtualization platform. As of now VMware NSX-v can be integrated with vSphere, vCloud Director, and vCloud Automation Center which gives fully-fledged network automation in private cloud. A multi-hypervisor environment, such as Xen server, KVM, or VMware ESXi with a choice of cloud management solution such as vCloud automation center, OpenStack, and CloudStack, can also be integrated with VMware NSX. This book features the **NSX-VMware** (**NSX-V**) version of NSX only. NSX-V will be referred to as NSX for the rest of the book.

The power of server virtualization and network virtualization

Server virtualization is the mainframe for the 21st century. A key use of virtualization in modern-day business is to consolidate the existing infrastructure to fewer physical machines. All companies have already virtualized their infrastructure since that is a potential game changer as we could consolidate servers and management, and deployment became much simpler. A hypervisor is a piece of software that allows us to run multiple virtual machines. The following are two types of hypervisors:

- **Bare metal**: Bare metal or type-1 hypervisors are pieces of software running directly on hardware, for example, VMware ESXi, KVM, Citrix XenServer, and Microsoft Hyper-V.
- **Hosted**: Hosted or type-2 hypervisors run on an existing operating system. Basically, they abstract guest operating systems from the host operating system, for example, VirtualBox, VMware workstation, and VMware player.

Similar to how a virtual machine is created, monitored, and deleted, NSX for vSphere offers logical switching, hypervisor level routing, virtual NIC-level firewall protection and Layer 4-Layer 7 load balancing service which can be provisioned, monitored, and deleted from a single pane of glass. As a result, a virtualized network is much more scalable and cost-effective compared with traditional physical network provisioning and management. Because of its native integration with other VMware products such as VRealize Automation and VCloud Director, a customer would use NSX in most of the VMware environments.

The following figure depicts server virtualization and network virtualization:

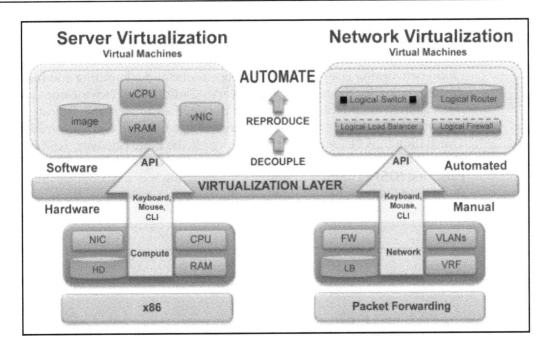

How to leverage NSX

When it comes to leveraging NSX features, customers have the following three options:

- Installing NSX in private cloud and leveraging NSX features.

  VMware NSX can be integrated with vSphere, vCloud Director, vCloud Automation Center and VMware Integrated Openstack. A multi-hypervisor environment, such as Xen Server, KVM or VMware ESXi™ with a choice of cloud management solution such as vCloud Automation Center.

- VMware vCloud Air, which is a public cloud, delivers advanced networking service networking and security features powered by NSX.

  Customer can secure networking in a public cloud built on the same platform as vSphere. Mirror on-premises networks in the cloud with minimal changes to design and networking topology. Manage at scale with controls and constructs familiar to network security administrators, minimizing operational disruption and need for retraining.

- For true network hybridity, a customer can have NSX in a private cloud and VMware vCloud Air as the public cloud.

  Cloud networking is an essential component of cloud computing and forms the foundation for the hybrid cloud. Every vCloud Air service includes a connection to the Internet, one or more public IP addresses, and critical networking capabilities such as load balancing, a firewall, **Network Address Translation** (**NAT**), and VPN connectivity via the Edge Gateway. NSX in vCloud Air supports **Border Gateway Protocol** (**BGP**) and **Open Shortest Path First** (**OSPF**) routing to simplify the integration of a customer's public cloud workloads and on-premises applications and resources.

A simple diagram describing the same is shown in the following figure:

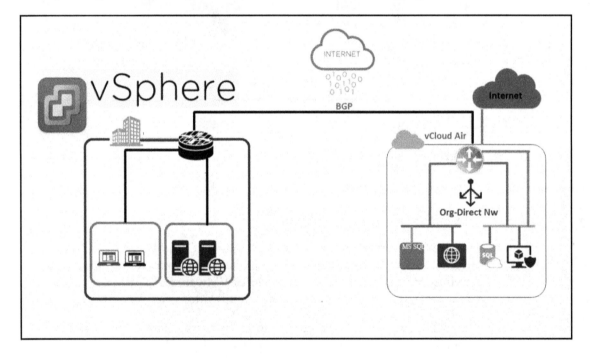

Feature-rich networking and security services on both private and public clouds ensure both the environments are secured and, most importantly, no application remodification is required while moving the workloads back and forth. The rest of the integration and design between private cloud with NSX and vCloud Air is beyond the scope of this book. We will have a quick look at NSX features and where they will fit in our current data center deployment scenarios.

It is very important to understand the nature of our application that is driving the network traffic in any data center environment. Traditional network architectures were based on a series of switches and routers, and those types of network architecture would perfectly fit in a client-server environment. Today's application workloads are highly in need of reducing the number of hops when they are communicating in a network. In modern-day application requirements, virtual machines talk to each other sitting in the same rack or a different rack before sending a reply packet to the client which is outside the data center. Workloads are moving from server memory to server flash drives for analysis. Big data, virtualization, and cloud have highly contributed to such types of traffic. Hence, we certainly need an intelligent networking for such big application workloads. Lack of speed and flexibility in provisioning a network is addressed with the help of network virtualization features.

With that said, let's have a look at the following diagram, which explains types of traffic in a data center environment. Networking traffic flow in a data center environment is of two types: **East-West** and **North-South**:

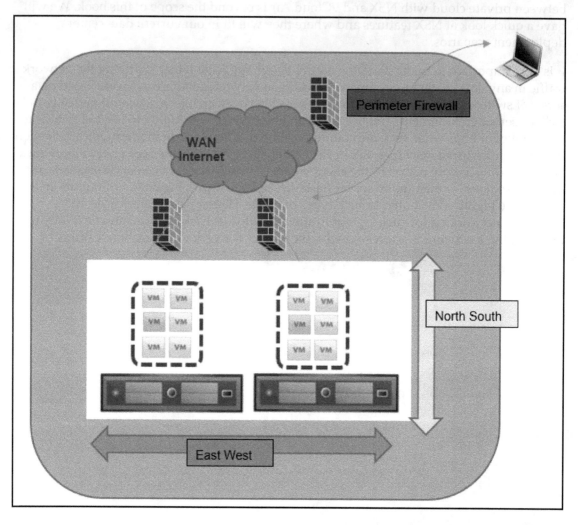

Let's have a look at an example. Let's assume we have a private data center and we need to access some applications which are hosted in a virtualized server from outside the data center:

- **East-West traffic**: Traffic between virtual machines in the same data center
- **North-South traffic**: Traffic which is coming into and going out of the data center

VMware NSX features

VMware NSX is the network virtualization platform for the **Software Defined Data Center** (**SDDC**), which is a completely non-disruptive solution as it reproduces the entire networking infrastructure in software which includes L2-L7 network services. NSX allows virtual networks to connect to physical networks by maintaining fine-grained security as per virtual NIC:

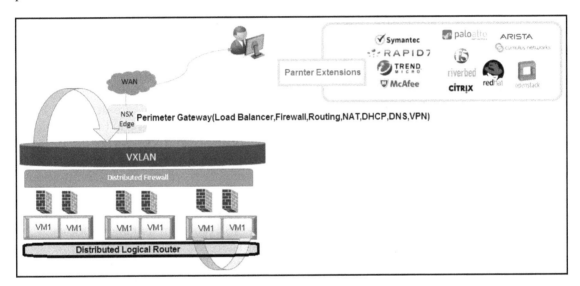

Let's discuss NSX features:

- **Logical switching**: NSX allows the ability to create logical switches which are nothing but vSphere port groups for workload isolation and separation of IP address space between logical networks. This means you are no longer limited to 4096 physical broadcast domains primarily because of VXLAN overlay networks. We will be discussing VXLAN during logical switch modules in more detail in Chapter 4, *NSX Virtual Networks and Logical Router*.

- **Gateway services**: The Edge Gateway service interconnects your logical networks with your physical networks. This means a virtual machine connected to a logical network can send and receive traffic directly to your physical network through the gateway. Edge Gateway provides perimeter services such as DHCP, VPN, dynamic/static routing, NAT, firewall, load balancing, DNS relay, and High Availability.

- **Logical routing**: NSX logical routing functionality allows a hypervisor to learn and route between different logical networks by limiting the North-South direction of traditional data center routing. Logical routers also can provide North-South connectivity, allowing access to workloads living in the physical networks. Both static and dynamic routing (OSPF, BGP, ISIS) are supported in NSX Edge.

- **Logical firewall**: Switching from a perimeter-centric security approach to per virtual machine level protection was not achievable till NSX was introduced. This has been of significant impact in on-demand cloud and VDI environments. Instead of sticking with traditional per data center level firewall protection, logical firewall gives per VM level protection and policies can be created, deleted with few clicks and policies remain intact even if virtual machines migrates from one host to another host. VMware NSX allows us to make use of a distributed logical firewall and an Edge firewall for use within your software-defined networking architecture. A distributed logical firewall allows you to build rules based on attributes that include not just IP addresses and VLANs but also virtual machine names and vCenter objects. The Edge Gateway features a firewall service that can be used to impose security and access restrictions on North-South traffic.

- **Extensibility**: Using the NSX extensibility feature, third-party VMware partner solutions can be integrated directly into the NSX platform that allows for a vendor choice in multiple service offerings. There are many VMware partners who offer solutions such as antivirus protection, IPS/IDS, and next-generation firewall services that can integrate directly into NSX, palo-alto for example. In addition to that, NSX admin can manage security polices and rules from a single pane of glass.

- **Load balancer**: NSX Edge offers a variety of network and security services and logical load balancer is one of them. There are two types of logical load balancer that NSX supports:
  - Proxy mode load balancer
  - Inline mode load balancer

  The logical load balancer distributes incoming requests among multiple servers to allow for load distribution while abstracting this functionality from end users. To ensure your application has the most up-time, we can configure the high availability feature for NSX Edge and that way it would be a highly available load balancer.

- **Dynamic Host Configuration Protocol (DHCP)**: NSX Edge offers DHCP services that allows for IP address pooling and also static IP assignments. An administrator can now rely on the DHCP service to manage all IP addresses in your environment rather than having to maintain a separate DHCP service. The DHCP service also can relay DHCP requests to your existing DHCP server as well. The NSX Edge DHCP service can relay any DHCP requests generated from your virtual machines to a pre-existing physical or virtual DHCP server without any interruptions.
- **Virtual Private Networks (VPN)**: The Edge offers the VPN service that allows you to create secure encrypted connectivity for end users to your applications and workloads hosted in private and public cloud. Edge VPN service offers SSL-VPN plus that allows for user access and IPSEC-policy-based site-to-site connectivity that allows for two sites to be interconnected securely.
- **Domain Name System Relay (DNS)**: NSX Edge offers a DNS service that can relay any DNS requests to an external DNS server.
- **Service composer**: Service composer allows you to provision and assign network security features to the applications hosted in a virtualized infrastructure. Network policies are automatically applied to virtual machines whenever they are added in virtual network.
- **Data security**: NSX data security provides visibility into sensitive data and ensures data protection and reports back on any compliance violations. A data security scan on designated virtual machines allows NSX to analyze and report back on any violations based on the security policy that applies to these virtual machines.
- **Trace flow**: Trace flow is a new feature added to NSX 6.2 which allows us to follow a packet from source to destination. Using the trace flow feature, we can monitor link utilization and troubleshoot network failures.
- **Flow monitoring**: Flow monitoring is a traffic analysis feature which provides a granular level of information in terms of number of packets transmitted per session, ports being used, and so on, and later an administrator can allow or block actions depending upon the output and business requirement.
- **Activity monitoring**: For detailed visibility per application, activity monitoring adds a lot of value. By doing so, an administrator will be able to monitor users and application-level information.

The features are summed up perfectly in the following block diagram:

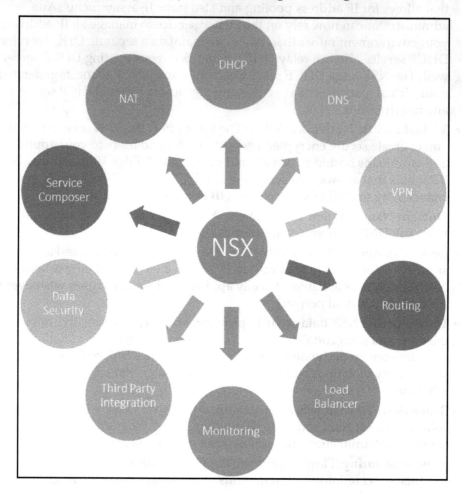

VMware NSX includes a library of logical networking services – logical switches, logical routers, logical firewalls, logical load balancers, logical VPN, and distributed security. You can create custom combinations of these services in isolated software-based virtual networks that support existing applications without modification, or deliver unique requirements for new application workloads.

 NSX 6.2.3 is the current NSX version at time of writing.

Summary

We started this chapter with an introduction to network virtualization and software-defined networking. We discussed concepts of network virtualization and introduced VMware's NSX network virtualization platform. We then discussed different NSX features and services, including logical switching, logical routing, Edge Gateway services, extensibility, service composer, and data security.

In the next chapter, we will discuss the NSX architecture.

2
NSX Architecture

In this chapter, we will have a high-level discussion on NSX architecture. To properly install and configure NSX, we should understand the core components that are involved in the NSX solution. By the end of this chapter, we will have a good understanding of the following aspects:

- Network planes
- NSX core components
- Identifying controller roles
- The controller cluster
- VXLAN architecture

Introducing network planes

In a traditional switch/router, routing and packet forwarding is ideally done on the same device. What does this mean? Let's take a classic example of configuring a router. We might configure SSH for managing the router and later configure routing protocols to exchange the routes with its neighbors. All these common tasks are done specifically on the same hardware device. So, in a nutshell, each and every router will take a forwarding decision based on the configuration of routers. The power of software-defined networking is decoupling the forwarding and control plane functionality to a centralized device called a controller and the end result is the controller maintaining the forwarding information and taking decisions rather than going via hop by hop in the traditional way. As shown in the following figure, the three functional planes of a network are the management plane, the control plane, and the data plane:

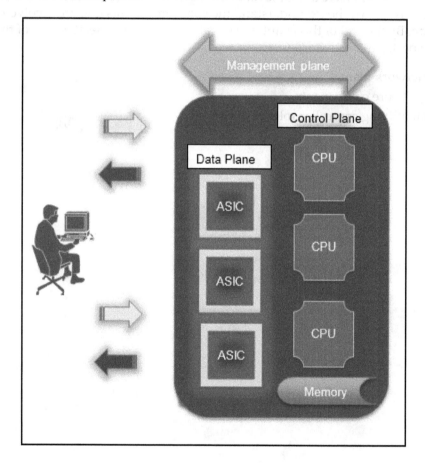

The three functional planes of a network are explained as follows:

- **Management plane**: The management plane is a straightforward concept: a slice of software through which we will make changes and configure network devices, and protocols such as SSH and SNMP are used to access and monitor them.
- **Control plane**: The classic example for the control plane is learning routes and making decisions based on routing algorithms. However, control plane functionality is not limited to learning routes. The control plane also helps in pairing with vendor-specific devices, and secures control plane access such as SSH and Telnet.
- **Data plane**: Data plane traffic is traditionally performed in dedicated hardware devices by consuming a little bit of compute resources. Primarily, the data plane is focused on data forwarding tasks.

I know most of us will be wondering why we are discussing network planes here. Network planes are DNA in the NSX world and we have all three planes which make the network virtualization layer.

NSX vSphere components

NSX uses the management plane, control plane, and data plane models. The components are represented diagrammatically in the following diagram:

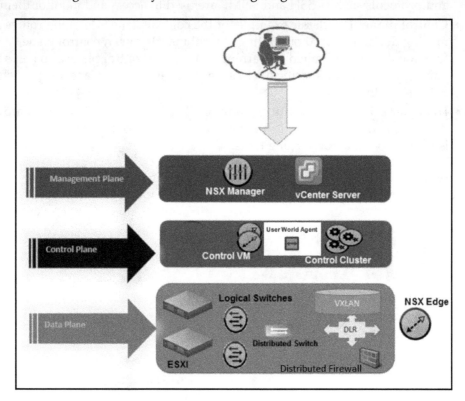

The management plane

The management plane contains the NSX Manager and vCenter Server. It is important to know that each NSX Manager should be registered with only one vCenter Server. The NSX Manager provides a management UI and API for NSX. We will be discussing NSX Manager and vCenter Server integration during NSX Manager installation and configuration modules. Once the integration is done, NSX Manager can be managed from a vSphere web client, which acts as a single pane of glass for configuring and securing the vSphere infrastructure. Immediate benefit is network administrators no longer need to switch between multiple management consoles. All network services can be configured and monitored from a single interface.

The control plane

The control plane primarily consists of NSX Controllers and the control VM, which allows us to perform distributed routing. The control plane also allows multicast-free VXLAN networks, which was a limitation in earlier vCloud networking and security versions. Controllers maintain ARP, VTEP (VXLAN tunnel endpoint), and MAC table. The NSX logical router control virtual machine and VMware NSX Controller are virtual machines that are deployed by VMware NSX Manager. The **User World Agent** (**UWA**) is composed of the ntcpad and vsfwd daemons on the ESXi host. Communication related to NSX between the NSX Manager instance or the NSX Controller instances and the ESXi host happen through the UWA. NSX Controller clusters are deployed in ODD number fashion and the maximum number of supported controllers is three. Since every controller in a control cluster is active at the same time, it ensures that the control plane is intact even if there is a controller failure. Controllers talk to each other to be in sync through a secured SSL channel. Controllers use a slicing technology to divide the workload among other controllers. Have a look at the following figure, which is a three-node controller cluster, in which slicing technology is dividing the workload across the controllers:

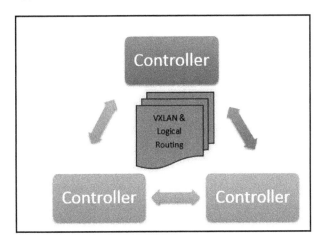

It is important to understand that there are two types of applications running on each of these controllers:

- **VXLAN**: Enables extension of a Layer-2 IP subnet anywhere in the fabric, irrespective of the physical network design.

- **Logical router**: Routing between IP subnets can be done in a logical space without traffic touching the physical router. This routing is performed directly in the hypervisor kernel with minimal CPU/memory overhead. This functionality provides an optimal data path for routing traffic within the virtual infrastructure.

The functionality of these applications is to learn and populate controller tables, and also distribute learned routes to underlying ESXi hosts. Lastly, the control plane and data plane configuration will be intact even during the failure of a management plane-this is the real power of software-defined networking.

Three-node controller clusters

In a large-scale distributed system with n number of servers, it is extremely difficult to ensure that one specific server can perform a write operation to a database or that only one server is the master that processes all writes. The fundamental problem is we do not have a simple way through which process execution can be done. How do we resolve this? All we need is to promote one server as master, and have some consensus with other servers. Paxos is a distributed consensus protocol published in 1989. The algorithm also ensures we have a leader election whenever there is a server failure. Paxos distinguishes the roles of proposer, acceptor, and learner, where a process (server/node) can play one or more roles simultaneously. The following are a few vendors who are using the Paxos algorithm extensively for the same reason:

- VMware NSX Controller uses a Paxos-based algorithm within an NSX Controller cluster
- Amazon Web Services uses the Paxos algorithm extensively to power its platform
- Nutanix implements the Paxos algorithm to ensure strict consistency is maintained in cassandara (for storing cluster metadata)
- Apache Mesos uses the Paxos algorithm for its replicated log coordination
- Google uses the Paxos algorithm for providing the Chubby lock service for loosely coupled distributed systems
- The Windows fabric used by many of the Azure services makes use of the Paxos algorithm for replication between nodes in a cluster

NSX Controllers are deployed in a three-node clustered fashion to ensure we are getting the highest level of resiliency since the controllers are running a fault-tolerant, distributed consensus algorithm called **Paxos**.

Controller roles

The NSX Controller provides the control plane functions for routing and logical switching functions. Each controller node is running a set of roles that defines the type of task the controller node can run. There are total of five roles running in a controller node; they are as follows:

- API
- Persistence server
- Logical manager
- Switch manager
- Directory server

While each of these roles needs a different master, it is important to understand that the leader is the responsible controller for allocating the tasks to other controllers.

The following figure depicts the responsibilities of various roles:

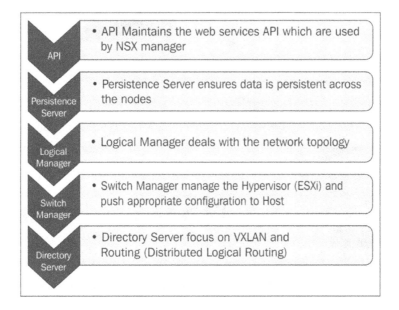

As we know, three node controllers form a control cluster. We will have a look at the role election per controller. Each role has a master controller node and only if a master controller node for a given role fails there would be a cluster-wide election for a new master role. This is one of the prime reasons a three-node cluster is a must in an enterprise environment, to avoid any split-brain situation which might eventually end up with data inconsistencies and the whole purpose of the control plane would be defeated. In the following figure, we have a three-node control cluster running and each controller is running a master role:

- **Controller 1**: Directory server master role running
- **Controller 2**: Persistence server master role running
- **Controller 3**: API and switch manager master role running

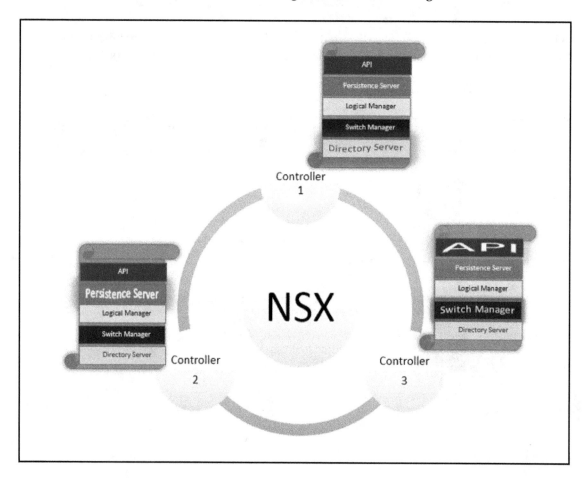

The data plane

NSX logical switches, ESXi hypervisor, distributed switches, and NSX edge devices are all data plane components. Once the management plane is up and running, we can deploy control plane and data plane software and components. Behind the scenes, these three**VMware Installation Bundles** (**VIB**) get pushed to the underlying ESXi hypervisor:

1. VXLAN VIB
2. Distributed routing VIB
3. Distributed firewall VIB

Up to now, we have discussed the management, control, and data plane components in the NSX world; in the upcoming modules, we will have a closer look at the installation part and design specification for each layer.

Overlay networks

A virtual network which is built on top of a physical network is called an overlay network. Does that sound familiar by any chance? Most enterprise environments would have used VPN technology for securing private or public networks, which is an IP-over-IP overlay technology. However, it is very important to understand that not all overlay networks are built on top of IP networks. The real question is, why do we require an overlay network ? As we can see from the following figure, we have two data centers and each of these data centers is following a spine-leaf topology. Flexible workload placement and virtual machine mobility, along with strong multitenancy for each tenant, are common asks in a virtualized infrastructure:

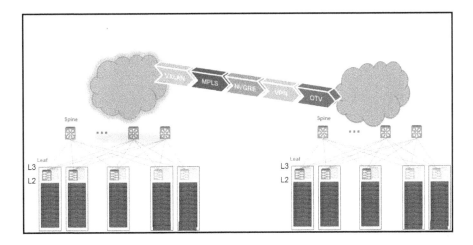

VXLAN, MPLS, NVGRE, VPN, and OTV are some of the classic examples of network-based overlays. Let's go back to the roots of server virtualization. Server virtualization virtualizes a physical server and allows multiple virtual machines to run on top of it with its own compute and storage resources. Now, each virtual machine might be having one or more than one MAC address, which eventually increases the MAC table in the network. Added to that, VM mobility forces the broadcast domains to grow. The traditional way of segmenting a network would be with the help of VLAN. As per the 802.1q standard, a VLAN tag is a 12-bit space providing a maximum of 4,096 VLANS. This is not a feasible solution in current multi tenant cloud environments wherein multiple machines reside on the same server and network isolation is required and workloads keep spiking, which demands a few VLANs to be provisioned for future growth and VLAN sprawl continues to happen based on workload mobility. Overlay networks alleviate this problem by providing Layer 2 connectivity independent of physical networks. We all know new technologies solve a lot of problems; however, there will always be challenges associated with them. Guess how difficult it will be for a network administrator to troubleshoot an overlay network! Trust me, when the mapping between the overlay network and physical network is crystal clear, it is extremely easy to perform troubleshooting. An NSX-VXLAN-based overlay network is a host-based overlay network which uses a UDP-based VXLAN encapsulation.

The VLAN packet

Before trying to understand VXLAN, let's go back to the fundamentals of a VLAN packet. How does tagging work in a VLAN packet? It's very simple concept: 4 bytes are inserted into the Ethernet header field (IEEE), which are a combination of a 2-byte **Tag Protocol Identifier** (**TPID**) and 2 bytes of **Tag Control Information** (**TCI**). The priority field is a 3-bit field that allows information priority to be encoded in the overall frame, 0 being the lowest priority and 8 the highest value. CFI is typically a bit used for compatibility between Ethernet and token ring networks and if the value is 0, those are Ethernet switches. Last but not the least, we have the VLAN field – VID:

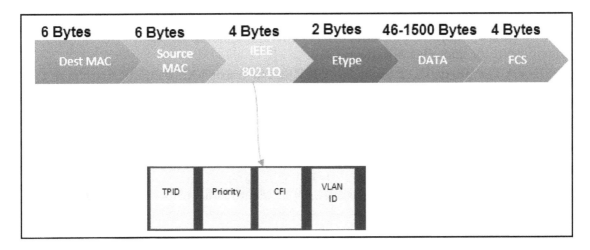

The act of creating a VLAN on a switch involves defining a set of switch ports, and end devices get connected to these ports. They all become part of that VLAN domain which eventually stops a broadcast not to be forwarded to another set of VLANs. I know whatever we have discussed so far is something which we will have heard in every networking class. This is just a repetition to ensure we never forget it. Now we can move on and discuss VXLAN.

A VXLAN overview

VXLAN is a technology developed by vendors such as Arista, VMware, Cisco, and Broadcom. Each of these VXLAN networks is called a logical switch (virtual wires in vCloud network security solution) and they are identified by a 24-bit segment-ID. In this way, customers can create up to 16 million VXLAN networks. **Virtual Tunnel End Points (VTEPs)** are the endpoints that encapsulate and de-encapsulate the VXLAN frames. Let's understand a few key terminologies in VXLAN; and we will discuss VXLAN frames after that:

- **VXLAN VIB**: VXLAN VIB or VMkernel modules are pushed to an underlying hypervisor during ESXi host preparation from NSX Manager.
- **Vmknic adapter**: Virtual adapter is responsible for sending ARP, DHCP, and multicast join messages. Yes, there would be an IP assigned (static/dynamic) to vmknic from the VTEP IP pool, which is one of the prerequisites for VXLAN configuration. NSX supports multiple VXLAN vmknics per host for uplink load balancing features.

- **VXLAN port group**: VXLAN port group is preconfigured during host preparation and it includes components and features such as NIC teaming policy, VLAN, and other NIC details.
- **VTEP proxy**: VTEP proxy is a VTEP that forwards VXLAN traffic to its local segment from another VTEP in a remote segment. NSX uses three modes of VXLAN: unicast, multicast, and hybrid. In unicast mode, VXLAN VTEP proxy is called UTEP and in hybrid mode, it is called MTEP.
- **VNI**: **VXLAN Network Identifier** (**VNI**) or segment ID is similar to VLAN-bit field; however, VNI is a 24-bit address that gets added to a VXLAN frame. This is one of the most critical elements in VXLAN frames, since it uniquely identifies the VXLAN network just as a VLAN ID identifies a VLAN network. VNI numbers start with 5000.
- **Transport zones**: Transport zones are basically a cluster or a group of clusters which define a VXLAN boundary or domain. Transport zones can be local or universal for multi VC deployment based on NSX design.

The VXLAN frame

The following are the main components of the VXLAN frame along with the figure:

- **Outer Ethernet header (L2 header)**: The destination MAC in the outer Ethernet header can be a next hop router MAC or destination VTEP MAC addresses and the source outer MAC address will be the source VTEP MAC address.
- **Outer IP header (L3 header)**: Respective VTEP source and destination IP will be populated in the outer IP header.
- **Outer UDP header (L4 header)**: The outer UDP header is a combination of source port and destination port. IANA has assigned the value 4789 for UDP; however, the VMware NSX default UDP port is 8472. So it is important to allow port 8472 in physical/virtual firewall devices for VXLAN traffic.
- **VXLAN header**: This is an 8-byte field which will have the VXLAN flag value, segment-ID, and reserved field:

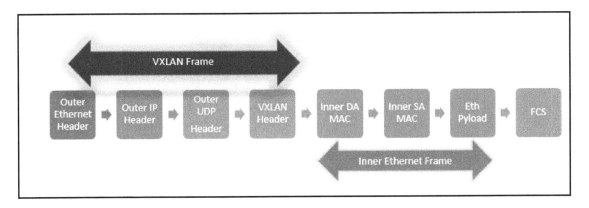

Since we have discussed the VXLAN packet format, let's move on and check the inner Ethernet frame.

The inner Ethernet frame

The following are the main components of the inner Ethernet frame along with the figure:

1. **Frame Check Sequence (FCS)**: FCS is a field at the end of the frame which is used to store the **cyclic redundancy check** (**CRC**) information. CRC is an algorithm which will run each time a frame is built, based on the data in the frame. When a receiving host receives the frame and runs the CRC, the answer should be the same. If not, the frame is discarded.

2. **Ethernet payload**: The length of a frame is very important, whether it is maximum or minimum frame size. The Ethernet payload field is a length field delimiting the length of the packet.

3. **Inner source MAC address**: The inner source MAC address will be the MAC address of the virtual machine which is connected to the VXLAN network.

4. **Outer destination MAC address**: The outer destination MAC address will be the MAC address of the destination virtual machine. Pause for a moment: what if a virtual machine doesn't know the destination virtual machine MAC? There is no rocket science here. All it does is a traditional broadcast, `ff:ff:ff:ff:ff:ff` (destination MAC), which is the broadcast address, and addresses every network adapter in the network and later this complete L2 frame will get encapsulated with the VXLAN frame before leaving the hypervisor host.

The life of a VXLAN packet

If we need to understand how a sequence of packets from a source machine reaches the destination in a unicast, multicast, or broadcast domain, all we do is a simple packet walk. In the following example, if **VM-A** is communicating with **VM-B** for the first time in a VXLAN domain, how is the encapsulation and de-encapsulation process happening?

The following diagram shows you how:

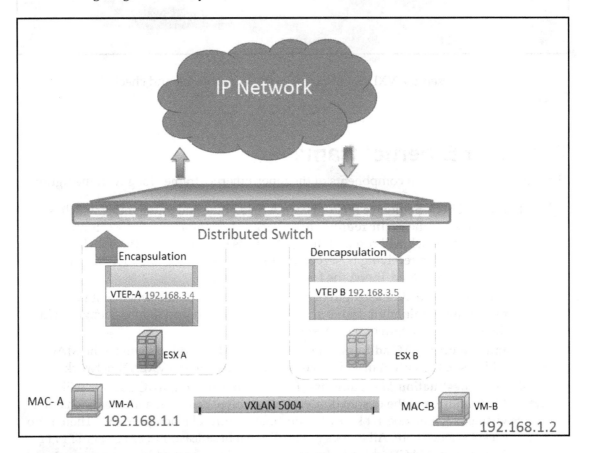

Let us now go through the steps one by one:

1. VM A-192.168.1.1, MAC- A on ESXi host A generates a broadcast frame (Layer 2 broadcast frame)
2. VTEP A on host A encapsulates the broadcast frame into UDP header with the destination IP as multicast/unicast IP based on VXLAN replication modes (Layer 2 header gets encapsulated with VXLAN header)

We will certainly have a discussion on VXLAN replication modes in Chapter 4, *NSX Virtual Networks and Logical Routing*.

3. The physical network delivers the packet to the host, because it was part of either the multicast group or unicast IP that we have defined during VXLAN replication modes.
4. VTEP B on ESXi host B will look at the VXLAN header (24-bit) and if matches with the VTEP table entries, it removes the VXLAN encapsulation header and delivers the Layer 2 packet to the virtual machine.

The preceding four steps mentioned are a simple packet walk on how virtual machines communicate in a VXLAN network. However, I haven't explained about ARP suppression and VTEP table learning because I want to explain that during NSX virtual networks and logical router.

Think for a minute and check in which scenario there won't be any encapsulation and de-encapsulation even though virtual machines are connected to a VXLAN network. No brainteasers here. If both the virtual machines are residing on same ESXi host and same VXLAN network, all it does is traditional Layer 2 learning and there is no encapsulation or de-encapsulation. These are very important points to note since it would ease a lot of troubleshooting issues when virtual machine to virtual machine communication is not happening due to VXLAN/physical network issues. I'm sure we have done such troubleshooting in vSphere environments.

Summary

We began the chapter with a brief introduction of NSX core components and looked at the management, control, and data plane components. We then discussed the NSX Manager and the NSX Controller clusters, which was followed by a VXLAN architecture overview discussion where we looked at the VLAN and VXLAN packet followed by a simple packet walk. Now we are familiar with the core components and their functionality.

In the next chapter, we will discuss NSX Manager installation and configuration.

3
NSX Manager Installation and Configuration

This chapter explains the list of prerequisites and installation steps for NSX Manager installation. The following are the key points that we will discuss:

- NSX Manager requirements
- NSX Manager installation
- NSX Manager design considerations
- Controller requirements
- NSX Controller deployments design considerations
- NSX data plane installation

NSX Manager requirements

VMware NSX Manager is a preconfigured virtual appliance which we can download from the VMware website just like any other VMware software. This preconfigured virtual machine comes with 16 GB of memory, 4 VCPUs, and 60 GB of storage space.

Let's have a quick look at the prerequisites for NSX Manager 6.2 installation:

- VMware vCenter server 6.0
- VMware ESXi 6.0
- Host clusters prepared with NSX 6.2
- vSphere distributed switch which is supported with the respective version of host and virtual center
- Ensure we have shared data stores through which we can leverage vSphere HA/DRS features to prevent downtime for NSX Manager VM
- Confirm whether we are using a dual stack or IPV4/IPV6 only networks
- Collect the Gateway, DNS, Syslog, and NTP server configuration
- All port requirements are updated in the VMware public knowledge base article at `https://kb.vmware.com/kb/279386`.

After downloading the NSX Manager OVA, we will follow the four-step process for installation and configuration of the manager software as listed in the following:

1. Deploy the NSX Manager OVA file
2. Log in to NSX Manager
3. Establish the NSX Manager and vCenter Server connection
4. Configure backup options

With that said, let's get started with the installation process. From my experience, I can confidently comment that deploying any appliances is a very easy task. However, when things start getting weird, we are forced to go back and review the deployment process and we find that the majority of the issues are something that we totally missed during the installation process wherein we just clicked the **Next**, and **Finish** buttons.

NSX Manager installation

For installing NSX Manager, perform the following steps:

1. Open vCenter via VMware web client.
2. Select **VMs and Templates**, right-click your data center, and select **Deploy OVF Template**.
3. Paste the VMware download URL or click **Browse** to select the file on your computer.
4. Click in the checkbox **Accept extra configuration options**.

> This allows you to set IPv4 and IPv6 addresses, default gateway, DNS, NTP, and SSH properties during the installation. If we do not set these configurations during deployment, we can always set them after the deployment.

5. Accept the VMware license agreements.
6. Edit the NSX Manager name (if required). Select the location for the deployed NSX Manager.
7. This name will appear in the vCenter Server inventory.
8. The folder you select will be used to apply permissions to the NSX Manager.
9. Select a host or cluster on which to deploy the NSX Manager appliance. I would prefer selecting a cluster and letting DRS decide the best host for placing the appliance.
10. Change the virtual disk format to **Thick Provision**, and select the destination data store for the virtual machine configuration files and the virtual disks.
11. Select the management port group for NSX Manager.

Finally, review the screen after all the options are configured and we can see that this is an IPV4 only deployment. So stay focused and review the screen once more and if any corrections are required, we should go back to previous steps and correct it.

Now that we have successfully deployed NSX Manager, it is worth double-checking all the configurations are intact and the manager appliance can ping DNS, NTP, Gateway, ESXi hosts, and VC. This is a very important step as any communication issues between manager and these components will have a direct impact on the functionality/deployment of VMware NSX features.

The following figure shows NSX Manager OVF details:

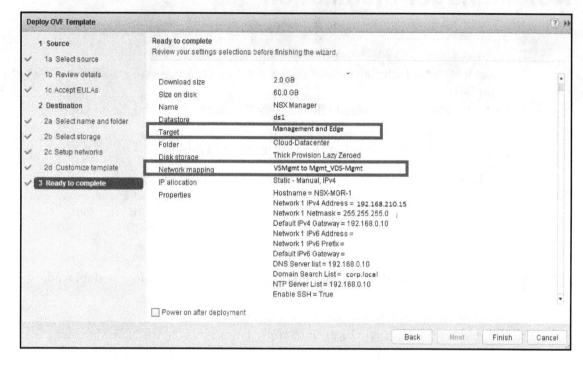

Let's make a note of the key configuration details from the preceding image and I will explain the design decisions for choosing it.

Understanding the key configuration details

As I said earlier, there are a few key design factors which we need to take care of while deploying NSX Manager appliances. Let's talk more about them.

Target – Management and Edge cluster

The management and edge cluster is a dedicated cluster in vSphere and it is always recommended to have a unique cluster for deploying all management components, which will ease any upgrade activity on the cluster without impacting the compute cluster, which is explicitly used for deploying end user virtual machines. In this example, we have a preconfigured vSphere cluster. And we leverage this cluster for deploying the following components:

- NSX Manager
- NSX Controller
- Vcenter Server
- Any other third-party or VMware management software

But remember that NSX can be integrated with a wide range of VMware products, such as Horizon View, SRM, vCloud Director, VRA, VIO, and VCO. So, based on the type of product integration and data center design, situations might demand having multiple management clusters for isolation purposes. For example, if we have two vCenter Servers in the primary site, one for vSphere with NSX integration and a second vCenter Server for SRM integration, it is okay to create two separate management clusters. Again, this is a design choice, whether we want all our eggs in one basket or we are okay to place them in unique baskets (cluster, rack).

Network mapping

We have connected NSX Manager to a vSphere distributed switch port group called **Mgmt_VDS_MGT**. These are preconfigured port groups which will be ideally configured with a VLAN port group. Either we can have a separate distributed switch for the management and edge cluster or we can have one single distributed switch which spans across multiple clusters. The preferred method of deployment would be having a unique distributed switch, as that would remain a VMotion boundary for management virtual machines. Yes, we don't want a **Distributed Resource Scheduler** (**DRS**) or manual migration movement for those virtual machines to any other compute cluster, as this would defeat the purpose of having a unique cluster for management and compute machines. Added to that, based on the physical network design, let's assume, as shown in the following screenshot, that we have a top-of-rack switch for the management and edge cluster which is running on a single rack. Any network-level changes in TOR switches have no impact on the compute cluster. Are we planning for LACP, static EtherChannel, or virtual PortChannel like configurations? It is important to note that the LACP configuration should be consistent across all port groups which are from the same distributed switch. The following diagram depicts a typical NSX enterprise vSphere design with separate compute and management and edge clusters:

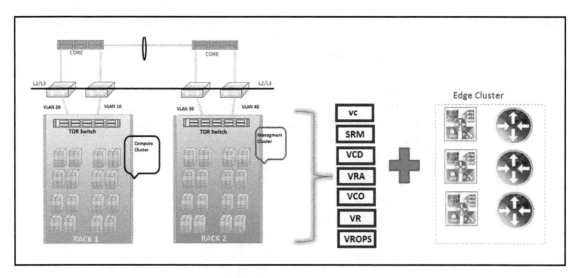

Compute and edge cluster with top of rack design

After confirming all our initial configurations are intact, we can log in to NSX Manager via a supported web browser, as shown in the following screenshot:

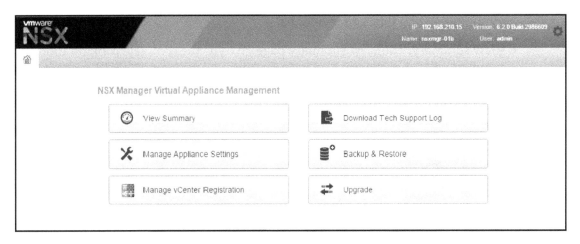

NSX Manager initial screen

From the preceding image, we can see the NSX Manager initial page and for me there is a significant difference between vCloud networking security and the NSX Manager initial page: all the options are well arranged with a straightforward explanation. By default, we can log in to NSX Manager using the following credentials. The default username and password for NSX Manager is as follows:

- User: admin
- Password: default

For security-hardening purposes, we can always change the password and create multiple users for management access. We can also see from the preceding image that on the right-hand side top corner, we have the initial configuration for NSX Manager along with the version of NSX, which is 6.2, and the build number.

NSX Manager virtual appliance management

Let's discuss different options that are listed in the preceding GUI. All these are key NSX appliance configuration and integration options:

- **View summary**: The view summary page gives us the complete configuration summary of NSX manager. This includes Virtual Appliance DNS, IP, version, and uptime/current time, along with common components and management services as shown in the following screenshot:

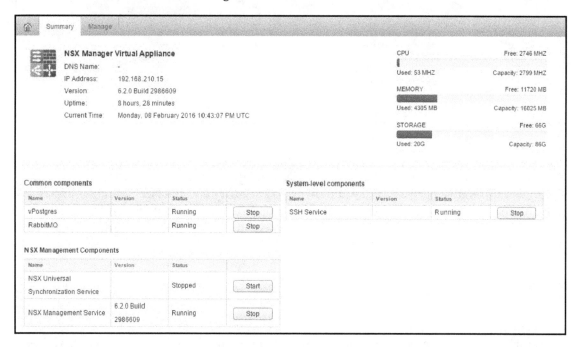

NSX Manager summary

One look at the preceding screenshot and we decipher that vPostgres, RabbitMQ, and management services should be up and running. **RabbitMQ** Server is a process which is hosted on NSX Manager and they interact with the **Firewall daemon (vsfwd)**, which is running on the ESXi host via the message bus. We will discuss vsfwd in more detail in Chapter 6, *Configuring and Managing NSX Network Services*; however, as of now we have to understand the importance of this service and how they communicate in the NSX world. Postgres is the NSX Manager database which comes along with the appliance. Hence, it is very important to note that any editing or table changes in the database through any methods will have a direct impact and it is highly recommended to perform such practices with the help of the VMware support team.

- **Manage appliance settings**: Manage settings will be extremely helpful to make any configuration changes against NSX Manager. For example, there is a new Syslog Server configured and we would like to leverage a new Syslog Server to be configured with the current NSX Manager. We can easily go ahead and update the changes by editing the **Syslog Server** tab. In earlier versions of NSX, SSL was disabled by default. However, starting from the NSX 6.1 release, SSL is enabled by default. So let's take a look at the following screenshot, which shows the **General** settings of NSX Manager:

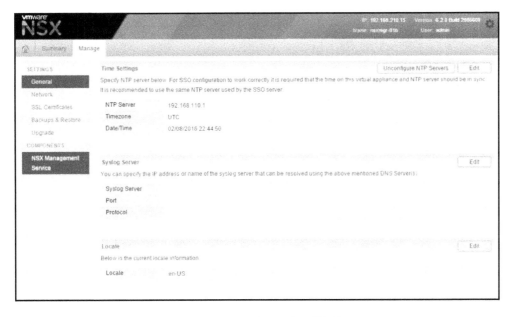

Time Settings, Syslog Server and Locale settings of NSX Manager

- **Manage vCenter registration**: NSX Manager and vCenter Server have a one-to-one relationship. With cross VCenter Server NSX installation, this is one of the most confused topics as we believe multiple VC is supported with a single NSX instance, which is totally wrong. NSX 6.2 allows you to manage multiple vCenter NSX environments from a single primary NSX Manager. Even in a Cross vCenter Server NSX installation, the NSX Manager to vCenter Server relationship is still one-to-one. More about cross VC installation will be discussed in Chapter 7, *NSX Cross vCenter*, NSX-vCross-vCenter feature and design decisions.

Register vCenter Server with NSX Manager

We will quickly go ahead and register NSX Manager with vCenter Server by following steps. The procedure for NSX Manager registration:

1. Firstly, log in to the NSX Manager virtual appliance.
2. Under **Appliance Management**, click **Manage Appliance Settings**.
3. We need to type the IP address of the vCenter Server.
4. Type the vCenter Server username and password.
5. Click OK.
6. Wait for few seconds for successful connection to the vCenter Server.

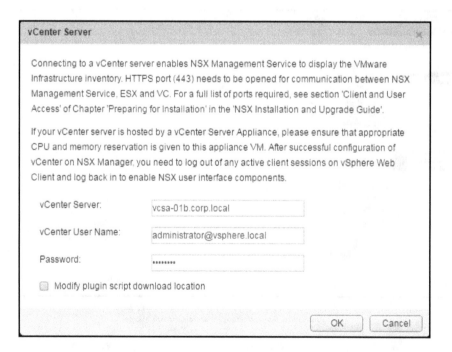

Register SSO with NSX Manager

For **single sign-on** (**SSO**) service integration with NSX, we need to configure the lookup service, which will improve the security of user authentication for vCenter users and enables NSX to authenticate from identity services such as AD, NIS, and LDA.

Procedure for LookUp service registration:

1. Log in to the NSX Manager virtual appliance.
2. Under **Appliance Management**, click **Manage Settings**.
3. Click **NSX Management Service**.
4. Click **Edit** next to **Lookup Service**.
5. Type the name or IP address of the host that has the lookup service.
6. Change the port number if required. The default port is **7444**.
7. The lookup service URL is displayed based on the specified host and port. Type the vCenter administrator user name and password.
8. This enables NSX Manager to register itself with the Security Token Service server.
9. Click **OK**.
10. Confirm that the lookup service status is connected.

The following figure shows successful registration of the lookup service and vCenter Server registration for NSX Manager:

It's time to explore other NSX Manager settings, such as Tech Support Logs, upgrading, and restoring the management appliance:

- **Download Tech Support Log**: For diagnostic purposes, we can go ahead and download the NSX Manager logs by clicking the **download** button under **NSX Manager virtual appliance management**.
- **Backup and Restore**: NSX Manager data, including system configuration, events, and audit log tables (stored in the Postgres DB), can be backed up at any time by performing an on-demand backup from the NSX Manager GUI. It is also possible to schedule periodic backups to be performed (hourly, daily or weekly).
- **Upgrade**: Based on the version of NSX Manager or vCloud network security solution, we will be in need of upgrading the management plane. Once we download the upgrade bundle, we need to upload the same to the **NSX Manager-Upgrade-Upload New Bundle** tab and click on **Upgrade**. Please note, upgrading NSX Managers won't upgrade control plane or data plane components.

Keep in mind that we are using an administrator role account to register the vCenter Server with NSX. Also note that on ASCII characters in the password will create synchronization issues with NSX Manager. A successful registration of NSX Manager with vCenter Server will let us manage NSX Manager via VMware web client and we will see **Networking & Security** solution in the web client inventory as shown in the following screenshot:

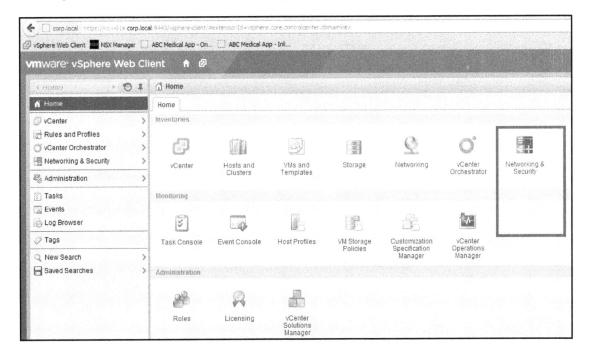

Lastly, let's go ahead and license NSX Manager.

Log in to the vCenter Server with the vSphere web client and perform the following steps:

1. In the middle pane, click the **Solutions** tab.
2. Select the **NSX** for vSphere solution.
3. Click the **Assign License Key** link.
4. In the **Assign License Key** panel, select **Assign a new license key** from the drop-down menu.
5. In the **License key** textbox, enter or paste your NSX for vSphere license key.
6. Click **OK**.

The VMware NSX for multi-hypervisor license key may also be used to license VMware NSX for vSphere.

NSX Manager deployment consideration

Due to the critical role NSX plays in a vSphere environment, it is extremely important to know and implement NSX management, control plane and data plane features. NSX management is NSX Manager, which provides a single point for configuring all NSX features and in addition we can leverage REST-API calls for deployment, configuration, and other tasks. So let's talk about communication channels from the management plane to other components.

The communication path

The following list shows the communication path between NSX Manager and various components:

- **NSX Manager to VCenter Server**: Communication between manager and VC is via vSphere API
- **NSX Manager to Controllers**: Communication between manager and controllers is via HTTPs
- **NSX Manager to ESXi hosts**: Communication between manager and underlying ESXi hosts would be via message bus.

Network and port requirements

NSX Manager virtual machines being part of the management plane, typically the NSX Manager and vCenter are placed on a single management network (vSphere PortGroup). I know most of the architects would be wondering having isolated networks (different subnets) for NSX Manager and vCenter Server will remain supported? The answer is *yes*, they can reside in different networks and also in different VLANs.

NSX for vSphere protocol and port requirements are updated as shown in the following screenshot:

Description	Port(s)	Protocol	Direction
NSX Manager Admin Interface	443	TCP	Inbound
NSX Manager REST API	443	TCP	Inbound
NSX Manager SSH	22	TCP	Inbound
NSX Manager VIB access	80	TCP	Inbound
NSX Manager vSphere Web Access to vCenter Server	443	TCP	Outbound
NSX Manager to Distributed Firewall	5671	TCP	Outbound
DNS client	53	TCP & UDP	Outbound
NTP client	123	TCP & UDP	Outbound
Syslog (Optional)	514	UDP or TCP	Outbound

Ensure that all these ports and protocols are allowed in the network.

User roles and permissions

Firstly, NSX roles and permissions are totally different from vCenter Server roles and permissions. Hence, it is important to secure user access. Using **Role Based Access Control (RBAC)**, we can secure a user access. Adding to that, we can also leverage vCenter SSO identity source users and groups once after properly configuring a lookup service with NSX Manager. NSX provides scope to restrict the area that a user can access in the NSX system:

- **Global**: The user has access to all areas of NSX
- **Limited access**: The user has access to only the NSX areas defined in the user profile

Various user roles are given as follows:

- **Enterprise Administrator:** NSX operations and security
- **NSX Administrator**: NSX operations only, for example, install virtual appliances, configure port groups, and so on
- **Security Administrator**: Read and write access to NSX security area, such as defining data security policies, creating port groups, and creating reports for NSX modules, and has read-only access to other areas
- **Auditor**: Has read-only access to all areas

A user cannot be defined without a role. After a role is assigned to users, the role can be changed. All these roles are extremely important when giving the permissions to NSX users and ensure we are giving limited access to non-enterprise administrator accounts.

Controller requirements

Now that we are clear about manager deployment and design decisions, let's discuss controller requirements. NSX Controllers are also deployed as virtual appliances with default compute resources per controllers. Since we have already registered NSX Manager with virtual center and ensured that we have ports and protocols opened, let me re-emphasize once again why controllers are required:

- VXLAN unicast and hybrid mode replication
- Distributed logical routing

Since NSX Controllers are virtual machines with control plane intelligence, from a network requirement perspective, they need to have an IP address. However, we don't stick with the traditional method of manual or DHCP discovery processes for IP assignments. Prior to controller deployment, let's configure IP pools.

The procedure for controller IP pool creation

IP pools are used for assigning IP addresses to controllers and **VXLAN Tunnel Endpoints** (**VTEP**). I certainly love this feature, which is a less manual process. All we need is to create an IP pool and the controller will pick an IP from the pool while it is getting created; also, it will release an IP during the deletion time:

1. From **vCenter Server Web Client**, navigate to **Networking Security** and under **Manage** select **Grouping Objects** as shown in the following screenshot:

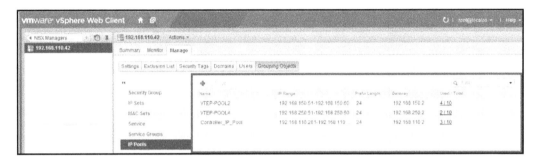

2. Click the + icon and we need to configure a static IP pool so that individual controllers can pick one IP from this pool as shown in the following screenshot:

3. Now that we have an IP pool ready, we can switch back to the NSX home installation page and click on the + sign under **NSX Controller Nodes** as shown in the following screenshot:

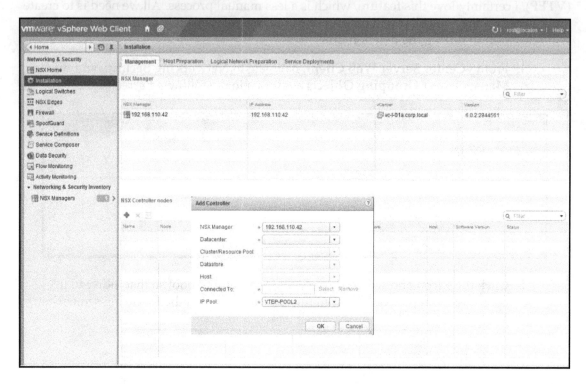

4. Select and update respectively **vCenter Datacenter**, **Cluster/Resource Pool**, shared **Datastore** location, vSphere PortGroup for connectivity, and lastly the name of **IP pool** which we created in step 2. After accomplishing the task, you'll see the following screenshot:

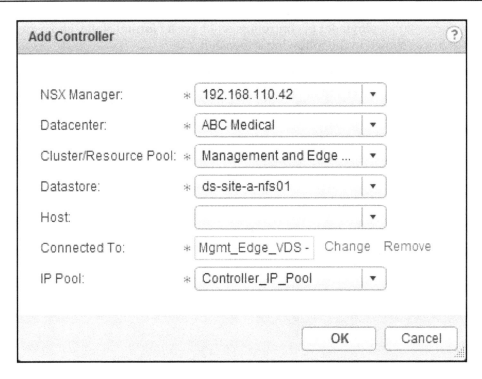

5. After the first controller is deployed, we can deploy an additional two more controllers by following the same steps since the three node control cluster is mandatory.

6. Successful deployment of controllers will have a **Normal** status and a green check mark as shown in the following screenshot:

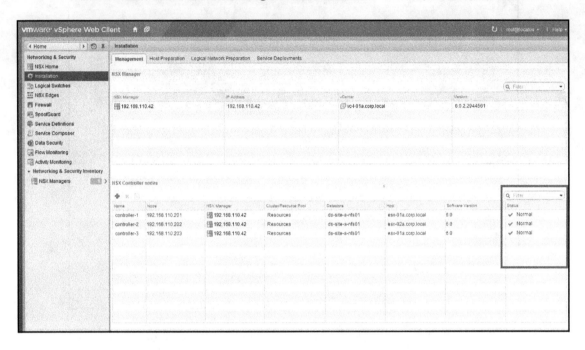

Let's make a note of all three controller IPs:

- **Controller 1**: 192.168.110.201
- **Controller 2**: 192.168.110.202
- **Controller 3**: 192.168.110.203

Even though we have controllers deployed and the status is green, it is important to check the control cluster connections and their status from the command line, which would give granular-level details. SSH to all three controllers and issue the following command:

```
Show Control-cluster status
# Command to Check Controller Status and ID
```

The controller types and their status are explained as follows:

- `Join status`: Verify the controller node is reporting join complete
- `Majority status`: Verify the controller is connected to the cluster majority
- `Cluster ID`: All the controller nodes in a cluster should have the same cluster ID

Remember the controller roles that we discussed in `Chapter 2`, *NSX Architecture*? Yes, those are the five roles which are populated here, as shown in the following screenshot – `api_provider`, `persistence_server`, `switch_manager`, `logical_manager`, and `directory_server`:

```
login as: admin
admin@192.168.110.201's password:
Linux nvp-controller 3.2.14-server-nn20 #1 SMP Fri Jan 4 02:02:34 PST 2013 x86_6
4
Nicira NVP Controller 3.2.1 (Build 29339)
show convp-controller # show control-cluster status
Type                Status                                  Since
----------------------------------------------------------------------------
Join status:        Join complete                           05/04 05:38:53
Majority status:    Connected to cluster majority           05/04 05:57:39
Restart status:     This controller can be safely restarted 05/04 05:57:29
Cluster ID:         6d31c240-5155-4c94-92f0-379f48e322ce
Node UUID:          6d31c240-5155-4c94-92f0-379f48e322ce

Role                Configured status  Active status
----------------------------------------------------------------------------
api_provider        enabled            activated
persistence_server  enabled            activated
switch_manager      enabled            activated
logical_manager     enabled            activated
directory_server    enabled            activated
nvp-controller #
```

Okay, this is all really great, but I know we have a few questions left. Let's have a look at those questions one by one.

How do we check which controller is master for those roles?

The following command will display that output for us:

```
Show Control-Cluster roles
```

Let's do a random check on one of those controllers, in this example, Controller 2, which is 192.168.110.202. As we can see from the following screenshot, except for the persistence server, all the roles are master in controller 192.168.110.202:

```
login as: admin
admin@192.168.110.202's password:
Linux nvp-controller 3.2.14-server-nn20 #1 SMP Fri Jan 4 02:02:34 PST 2013 x86_6
4
Nicira NVP Controller 3.2.1 (Build 29339)
Last login: Fri May  6 06:07:16 2016 from 192.168.110.10
nvp-controller # show control-cluster roles
                         Listen-IP  Master?    Last-Changed  Count
api_provider         Not configured      Yes  05/06 06:18:54      3
persistence_server              N/A       No  05/06 06:18:54      4
switch_manager       Not configured      Yes  05/06 06:18:54      3
logical_manager                 N/A      Yes  05/06 06:18:54      3
directory_server                N/A      Yes  05/06 06:18:54      3
nvp-controller #
```

SSH session NSX Controller

The controller cluster majority leader listens on port 2878 and will have a Y in the listening column. To check that, let's issue the following command and check on the same controller 192.168.110.202 that we have checked during step 2:

Show Control-Cluster Connections

We got the following output:

```
nsx-controller # show control-cluster connections
role                    port             listening open conns
----------------------------------------------------------------
api_provider            api/443          Y         4
----------------------------------------------------------------
persistence_server      server/2878      -         0
                        client/2888      Y         1
                        election/3888    Y         0
----------------------------------------------------------------
switch_manager          ovsmgmt/6632     Y         0
                        openflow/6633    Y         0
----------------------------------------------------------------
system                  cluster/7777     Y         1
nsx-controller #
```

Does that look bit weird?

We know that the controller cluster majority leader listens on port `2878` and would have a –
in the `listening` column for persistence server for controller `192.168.110.202`. No
rocket science here; as per the `Show Control-Cluster roles` output which we have
tested in step 7, except for the persistence server role, for the rest of the roles, controller
cluster 2 was master, hence `Show Control-Cluster Connections` is reporting – for the
persistence server. I hope we now have some basic understanding of controller roles. We
will discuss a few troubleshooting scenarios in `Chapter 8`, *NSX Troubleshooting*.

NSX Controller design consideration

NSX Controller virtual machines are the DNA of the control plane, hence it is important to
take decisions on where to install and connect the controller. Lastly, we don't want the
controller to get exposed to users who are leveraging NSX features; basically, no control
plane attack.

Communication path

It's good to know the communication protocol used between NSX Manager, controllers and
NSX Edges:

- Communication between controller and NSX Manager – HTTPS
- Communication between Edge and controller – HTTPS

Network and port requirements

Ensure that the port requirements mentioned in the following screenshot are met for controller communication:

Description	Ports	Protocols	Direction
Controller-SSH	22	TCP	Inbound
Controller-API	443	TCP	Inbound
Controller-ESXI(UW agent)	1234	TCP	Outbound
DNS	53	TCP/UDP	Outbound
NTP	123	TCP/UDP	Outbound
Controller-Controller	3888,2888,7777,30865	TCP	Outbound

Controller deployment consideration

I know, I keep telling you this: the real power of NSX is all about controllers. How we deploy our controllers, what best practices are implemented, all makes a vital difference in NSX design. You know by now, because of overlay networks, there will be a whole bunch of design best practices that we might need to do in both the physical and virtual worlds. But here, we will discuss controller deployment considerations:

- First and foremost, NSX Controllers should be deployed in the same vCenter where NSX Manager is registered. The only exception would be while leveraging cross-VC NSX design, which we will discuss in Chapter 7, *NSX Cross vCenter*.
- While deploying the controllers, don't make any other configuration changes or deploy any other NSX features. The rule is the same even if we are deleting a controller and deploying a new one during break fix scenarios.
- Use a separate vSphere Edge cluster for controller deployments. For small-scale deployments, it is okay to deploy controllers in a management cluster.
- NSX Controllers should be reachable with all ESXi host vmkernel networks and NSX Manager management networks.

- The controller being a VM, most of the enterprise environments will have the vSphere **Distributed Resource Schedular** (**DRS**) feature and it will consider it as a normal virtual machine and will migrate or place it on same ESXi host based on the placement algorithm. To ensure controllers are not getting deployed or migrated to the same host and if there is a host failure this will have a direct impact on controllers and the entire control plane will be down. To avoid such situations, we will have to leverage vSphere anti affinity rules to avoid deploying more than one controller on the same ESXi host. Adding to that, I would highly recommend starting with more than three host clusters and later scale accordingly. This way, we can easily place controllers on separate ESXi hosts and scale accordingly. Don't get my message wrong, we are deploying three controllers on three different hosts and not leaving the rest of the host as a spare one. In any environment, we will be doing maintenance activity, sometimes as a part of a software upgrade or maybe adding or removing hardware devices from the server. For such scenarios, when we take a downtime for one of the hosts, we are still left with more than three ESXi hosts and controllers would be placed on them based on the anti affinity rules.
- All the hosts in the cluster should have automatic VM startup/shutdown enabled.

 The first host where the controllers are deployed will have automatic VM startup/shutdown enabled by default.

That summarizes controller deployment and key design aspects. With that, let's move to data plane preparation. Time to memorize what we did so far? Yes, let's do it. We have deployed NSX Manager (management plane) and registered the solution with vCenter Server. Later, we deployed NSX Controllers (control plane) and, finally, we are in the last phase of installation, which is the data plane.

The NSX data plane

The NSX data plane consists of **vSphere Distributed Switch** (**VDS**), kernel modules, User World Agents, NSX Edge, and Distributed routing/firewall and bridging modules. Firstly, let's discuss preparing ESXi clusters for NSX.

What is host preparation? All it does is install the kernel modules and builds a management and control plane domain. The kernel modules that we refer to here are as follows:

- Distributed routing
- Distributed firewall
- VXLAN bridging

In a multi-cluster environment, we need to perform this installation per cluster level. Based on the vSphere design, we can always introduce new hosts to the cluster and preparation is automated for newly added hosts, which makes life easier for architects.

The host preparation procedure

Let's discuss how an ESXi host is prepared to push the kernel modules:

1. In vCenter, navigate to **Home** | **Networking & Security** | **Installation** and select the **Host Preparation** tab.
2. Select the respective cluster and click the gear icon and click **Install** as shown in the following screenshot:

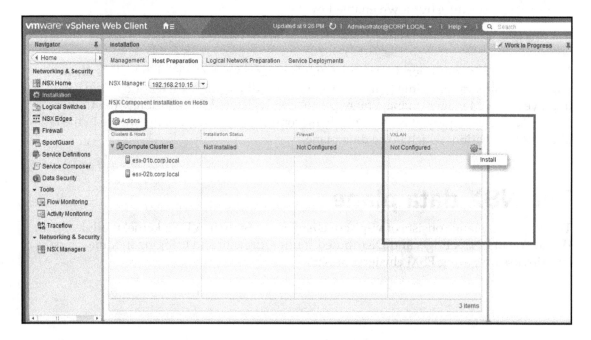

3. Monitor the installation. Repeat the same steps for other clusters.

   Now, one common question from all vSphere folks: do we need to reboot the host since VIBS got installed? The answer is a **BIG FAT NO**! Only after uninstallation scenarios do we need a host reboot. We humans tend to forget things easily, don't we? No problem, there would be a message populated near our ESXi host icon notifying *Reboot Required*.

4. For each vSphere cluster, we will go ahead and configure **VXLAN** networking prerequisites.

Firstly, we will configure a **static pool** for the **VTEP IP** assignment, which is similar to the controller **IP pool** configuration that we did earlier. The **DHCP** pool assignment is also possible; however, in this case, I'm showcasing the IP assignment with static pools.

From NSX Manager, navigate to manage **IP pools** and click on the + sign. Update the following:

- VTEP **Name**
- **Gateway** address
- **Prefix Length**
- **Static IP Pool** for VTEP IP assignments.

Have a look at the following screenshot for reference:

Select one of the vSphere clusters and click the configure link provided in the VXLAN column:

1. Select the vSphere distributed switch.
2. Update the **VLAN** number. Enter if you're not using a VLAN, which will pass along untagged traffic.
3. Ensure **MTU** is **1600** (VXLAN overhead)
4. For VMKnic IP addressing, we need to make use of the earlier VTEP IP pool that we configured.

VMKNic Teaming Policy method is used for bonding the vmnics (physical NICs) for use with the VTEP port group. I have selected for fail over. The other options are Static EtherChannel, LACP (Active), LACP (Passive), Load Balance by Source ID, Load Balance by Source MAC, and Enhanced LACP. The following screenshot is updated with a list of supported VXLAN NIC teaming policies:

Teaming & Failover Mode	NSX Support	Multi VTEP	Uplink Behavior
Route Based on Originating Port	YES	YES	Both Active
LACP	YES	NO	Flow Based-Both Active
Route Based on Source MAC hash	YES	YES	Both Active
Route based on IP HASH	YES	NO	Flow Based-Both Active
Explicit Failover	YES	NO	Only 1 Active
Route Based on physical NIC load(LBT)	NO	NO	NO

VTEP NIC teaming design is extremely critical in NSX environments. Most customers would go with single VTEP configuration primarily because of the simplicity in the design. However, if we have more than 10G VXLAN traffic, LACP or Static EtherChannel would be the preferred load balancing policy.

VTEP Value is the number of VTEPs per host. Is there any specific reason why we would go for multi VTEP configuration? Well, if we have more than one physical link that we would like to use for VXLAN traffic and the upstream switches do not support LACP the use of multiple VTEPs allows us to balance the traffic between physical links.

The following screenshot depicts the preceding step:

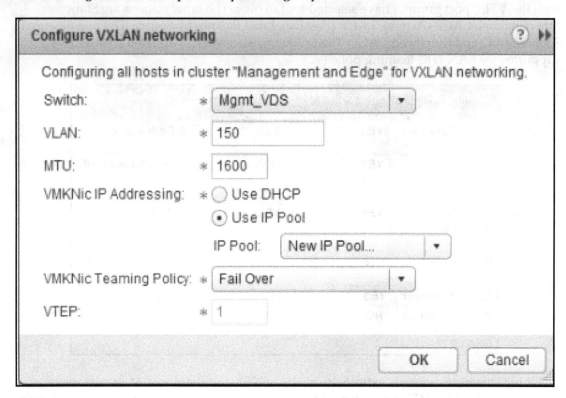

Based on the requirement, we can repeat the same step for other clusters as well, and each such configuration will create a VXLAN distributed port group in vSphere.

Successful installation of VXLAN modules will show as **Configured** as highlighted in the following screenshot:

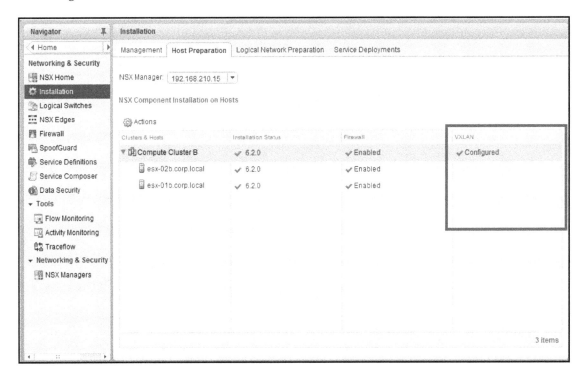

I know most us will have a few design-related queries on VXLAN and how it works. Stay focused: we are going in the right direction and will discuss that in upcoming chapters.

Summary

We started this chapter with an introduction to NSX Manager requirements and we covered all design aspects of the management plane. Later, we discussed NSX Controller requirements and key design decisions. Finally, we moved to data plane installation. In the next chapter, we will discuss managing and deploying NSX logical networks.

4

NSX Virtual Networks and Logical Router

Scalability and flexibility are impressive features of Network Virtualization. On any IP network, any Switches/Routers, any physical network design NSX works flawlessly. With the emerging interest in overlay networks, there are different encapsulation technologies currently in the market. VXLAN, NVGRE, LISP are few in that list. In this chapter we will discuss on logical networks and how NSX simplifies datacenter routing and switching. Following topics will be the key points:

- NSX logical switches
- NSX virtual network creation – multicast, unicast, and hybrid replication modes
- NSX virtual network best practices and deployment considerations
- NSX logical router
- NSX logical routing and bridging best practices

NSX logical switches

Using VMware NSX virtual networks, we can create a logical network on top of any IP network. We have already discussed VXLAN fundamentals and the host installation process in the previous chapters. Now that we have a good understanding of the basics, it's time to move on with virtual network creation. Before we begin exploring, it is important to understand that each logical network is a separate broadcast domain.

Logical network prerequisites

Firstly, let's have a look at the prerequisites for logical network creation:

- Host preparation
- Segment ID (VNI) pool
- Global transport zone

Host preparation

We have already discussed in detail how the underlying ESXi host is prepared from NSX Manager in `Chapter 3`, *NSX Manager Installation and Configuration*. Here, it is time to recollect that knowledge.

The hypervisor kernel modules enable ESXi hosts to support VXLAN, the logical switch, the distributed router, and the distributed firewall.

Segment ID (VNI) pool

As we know, the VXLAN network identifier is a 24-bit address that gets added to the VXLAN frame, which allows us to isolate each VXLAN network from another VXLAN network.

Steps to configure the VNI pool

Here are the steps to configure the VNI pool:

1. On the **Logical Network Preparation** tab, click the **Segment ID** button.
2. Click **Edit** to open the **Edit Segment IDs and Multicast Address Allocation** dialog box and configure the given options.
3. Click **OK** as shown in the following screenshot:

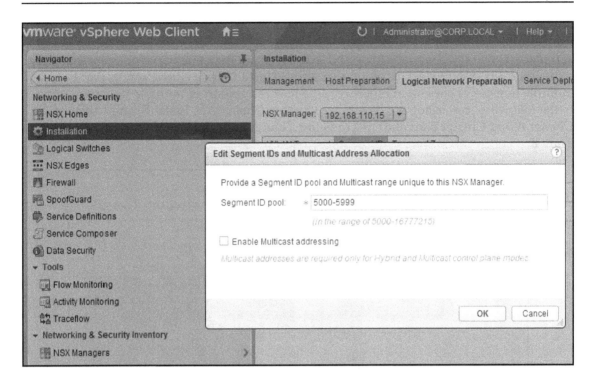

In this example, we are not using multicast networks; rather, we want to leverage unicast networks. One of the classic examples of multicast VXLAN networks would be when a customer has existing VXLAN networks (created when he was using vCloud network security) and the management software was upgraded to NSX. For such a scenario, people stick with multicast mode VXLAN networks in NSX. Also, please note that we don't even need a controller in that case. Do not use 239.0.0.0/24 or 239.128.0.0/24 as the multicast address range, because these networks are used for local subnet control, meaning that the physical switches flood all traffic that uses these addresses. The complete list is documented at `https://tools.ietf.org/html/draft-ietf-mboned-ipv4-mcast-unusable-1`.

Transport zone

A transport zone is a boundary for a VNI. All clusters in the same transport zone share the same VNI. A transport zone can contain multiple clusters and a cluster can be part of multiple transport zones or, in other words, a host can be part of multiple transport zones. In the following screenshot, we have three clusters: **Cluster A**, **Cluster B**, and **Cluster C**. **Cluster A** and **Cluster B** are part of **Transport Zone A** and **Cluster C** is part of **Transport Zone B**.

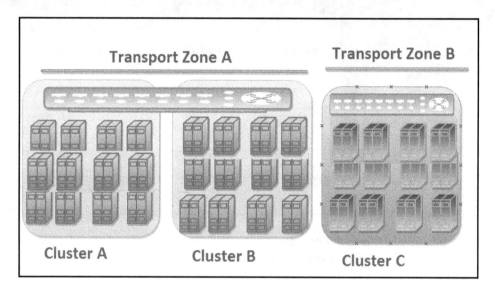

Configuring a global transport zone

The following steps will help you to configure the transport zone:

1. On the **Logical Network Preparation** tab, click **Transport Zones**.
2. Click the green plus sign to open the **New Transport Zone** dialog box and configure the following options and click **OK**:
    *   Enter the transport zone name in the **Name** text box.
    *   In **Control Plane Mode**, select the **Unicast**, **Multicast**, or **Hybrid** button.
    *   In **Select clusters to add**, select the check box for each of the vSphere clusters listed. Also, have a look at the distributed switch selection highlighted in red. We are following one of the NSX-DVS design best practices. Both the compute clusters are running on **Compute_VDS** and the management cluster is on **Mgmt_Edge_VDS**.

2. Once it is updated, verify that the transport zone appears in the transport zone list, with a control plane mode set to unicast, multicast, or hybrid based on the preceding selection. Refer to the following figure:

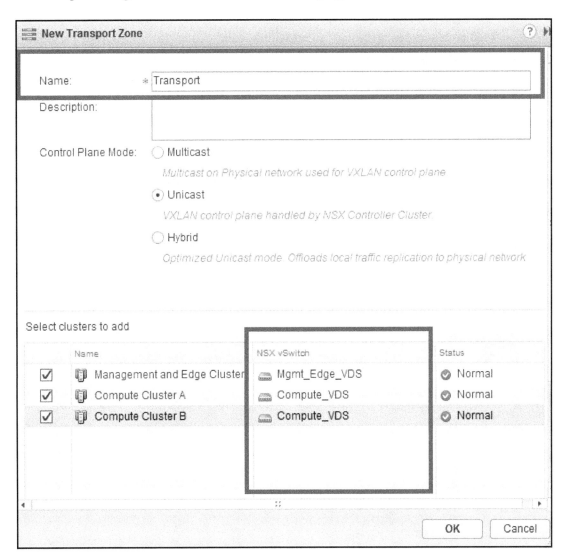

We have now completed all the prerequisites for NSX logical networks. In this example, we have the following virtual machines already created in vSphere without any network connectivity. We will go ahead and create four logical networks and will connect to virtual machines and later we will test connectivity:

- **Two web servers**: web-sv-01a and web-sv-02a
- **One DB server**: DB-sv-01a
- **Application server**: app-sv-01a

Creating logical switches

In an old-fashioned vSphere environment, ideally, virtual machines will be connected to a preconfigured vSphere PortGroup with or without VLAN tagging. But now we are in the NSX world and let's leverage an NSX logical switch for virtual machine connectivity. In the left navigation pane, select **Logical Switches** and in the center pane, click the green plus sign to open the **New Logical Switch** dialog box. Perform the following actions to configure the logical switch:

1. Enter App-Tier in the **Name** text box.
2. Verify that the **Transport Zone** selection is **Transport**.
3. Verify that the **Control Plane Mode** selection is **Unicast**.
4. Click **OK**:

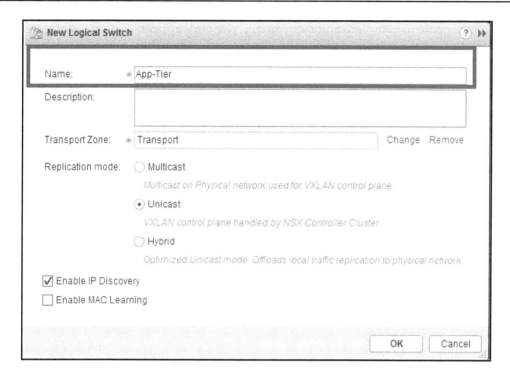

The following are the two options shown on the **New Logical Switch** screen:

- **Enable IP Discovery**: Another great feature, which minimizes ARP flooding in a VXLAN network. When a virtual machine sends an ARP packet, the switch security module – which is nothing but a dvfilter module attached to VNIC – will query the NSX Controller to know if they have the MAC entry for that destination IP. Everyone knows that we have two chances in that case:
  - The controller has the MAC entry
  - The controller doesn't have the MAC entry
  - In the first condition, since the controller has the MAC entry, it will respond with the MAC address and, that way, ARP traffic is reduced. In the second condition, the controller responds with no MAC reply and the ARP will flood in the normal way.
- **Enable MAC Learning**: When we enable MAC learning a VLAN/MAC pair table is maintained on each vNIC which is used by dvfilter data. This table will be intact whenever VM migrates from one host to another host with the help of dvfilter data.

Wait for the update to complete and confirm app-network appears with the status set to **Normal**. Repeat Steps 1-4 and create three more logical switches, and name them **Web-Tier**, **DB-Tier**, and **Transit** networks. The successful creation of logical switches will show us the same results when populated under logical switches, as shown in the following screenshot:

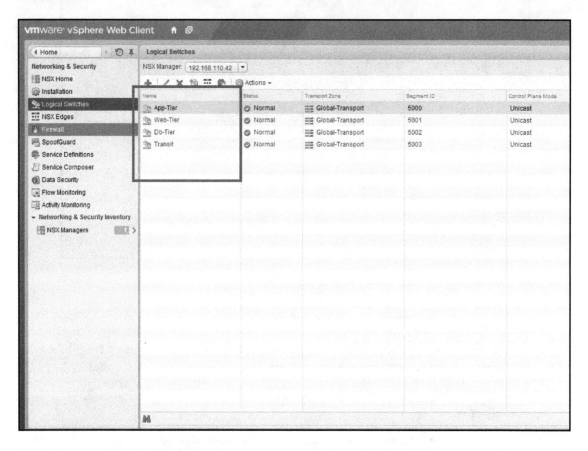

With the preceding steps, we see four port groups created in the vSphere networking option with their respective VNI-ID:

- **5000**: **Transit** network
- **5001**: **Web_Tier** network
- **5002**: **App_Tier** network
- **5003**: **DB_Tier** network

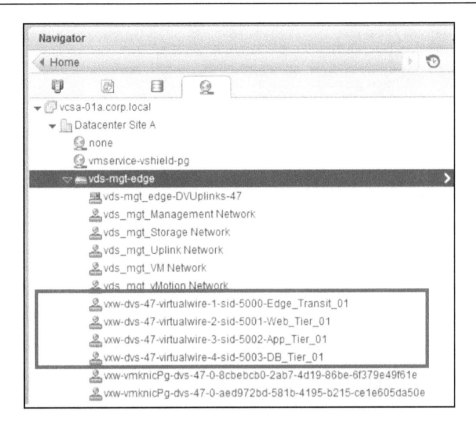

Understanding replication modes

Let's discuss replication modes in more detail and later we will connect the logical switches to virtual machines. With the addition of an NSX Controller, the requirement for multicast protocol support on physical networks is completely removed for VXLAN. There are three replication modes:

- **Multicast**: When multicast replication mode is chosen for a given logical switch, NSX relies on the Layer 2 and Layer 3 multicast capability of the data center physical network to ensure VXLAN encapsulated multi-destination traffic is sent to all the VTEPs. This mode is recommended only when you are upgrading from older VXLAN deployments (vCloud network security). It requires PIM/IGMP on a physical network.

- **Unicast**: The control plane is handled by the NSX Controller. All unicast traffic leverages head end replication. No multicast IP address or special network configuration is required. In unicast mode, the ESXi hosts in the NSX domain are divided into separate VTEP segments based on the IP subnet their VTEP interfaces belong to. There will be a UTEP selection for each segment to play the role of **Unicast Tunnel End Point (UTEP)**. The UTEP is responsible for replicating multi-destination traffic received from the ESXi hypervisor hosting the VM sourcing the traffic and belonging to a different VTEP segment from all the ESXi hosts part of its segment.
- **Hybrid**: The optimized unicast mode. Offloads local traffic replication to a physical network (L2 multicast). This requires IGMP snooping on the first-hop switch, but does not require PIM. The first-hop switch handles traffic replication for the subnet.

We will consider the following screenshot as a network topology and will explain all three modes of replication, which will give us a precise picture of how replication works:

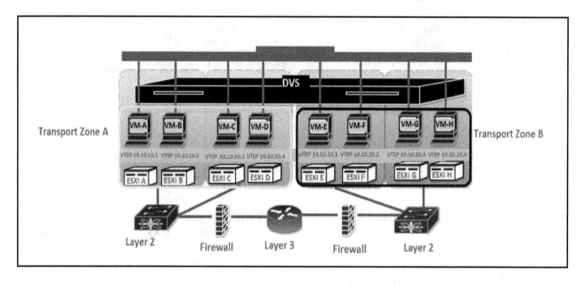

Firstly, let's understand the configuration. The preceding screenshot shows us the following:

- There are two transport zones in this set-up, **Transport Zone A** and **Transport Zone B**
- A **Distributed Virtual Switch (DVS)** is part of both the transport zones
- All the virtual machines are connected to one common VXLAN network – **VXLAN 5001**

We will walk through all the modes one by one and also discuss their design decisions in the following sections.

Unicast mode packet walk

Let's discuss a unicast mode VXLAN packet walk:

- **VM-A** generated **Broadcast, Unknown Unicast, Multicast (BUM)** traffic, which is typically Layer 2 traffic.
- **ESXi-A** will do a local VTEP lookup and will learn that the packet needs to be locally replicated (same subnet), in this case **ESXi-B**.
- In addition to that, the packet will also get remotely replicated. Since we have four hosts in a remote subnet (ESXi E, F, G, and H), to which host will it send the packet? This is one key differentiator between multicast mode VXLAN and unicast. In unicast mode, the packet will be sent to a proxy module called **UTEP** with a replicate-locally bit set. Why is it like that? The answer is very simple: since there is a replicate-locally bit set, UTEP will replicate the packet locally to one of the ESXi hosts that are part of same subnet. In this example, we have two subnets; based on the network topology, the process will be same for every subnet.

Design decisions for unicast mode VXLAN

There is not much to be discussed about unicast mode VXLAN design. However, it is important to know the following points:

- We could simply stick with traditional IP network design and just ensure that the MTU is increased to 1,600.

- Let's go back and read the VXLAN packet walk in unicast mode; what does it do in a nutshell? It replicates the packet locally and sends one copy to the remote subnet and again replicates it locally. Who does that replication? The ESXi host does all this intelligent work and of course, based on how big the environment is or how often we have **BUM** traffic, it will create a slight overhead on the hypervisor. So I would suggest unicast mode as the best way to start using VXLAN; however, it is not a great candidate for large environments.
- In environments where customers have multicast limitation, unicast mode VXLAN is best.

Multicast mode packet walk

Whenever I used to explain about multicast VXLAN networks, it made me recollect the VMware **vCloud Networking and Security** (**vCNS**) solution days. Multicast mode VXLAN was the starting stage of VXLAN implementation in both virtualized vSphere environments and cloud environments running on vCloud director software. The solution was very powerful; however, physical network prerequisites were one of the difficult factors for all architects because it really defeats the purpose of saying NSX can be run on any IP network. The bitter truth is that IP networking demands some requirements for the technology to work flawlessly. With that said, let's start with a packet walk:

- **VM-A** generates **BUM** traffic.
- **The ESXi A** host encapsulates the packet with a VXLAN header (5001). Time to start guessing who it will send the packet to. Will it simply be broadcast? The Layer 2 frame is a broadcast frame encapsulated with a VXLAN header; however, the host would be sending it to one of the multicast groups. How will we ensure the multicast reaches only **ESXi B**, **E**, **F**, **G**, and **H** since we have a virtual machine running on the same VXLAN network? This is where a physical network requirement is a must. We need IGMP snoop for that; if not, that would be treated as an unknown multicast packet.
- The **router** will perform an L3 multicast and will send it to a Layer 2 switch and the switch will again check the multicast group and will send it to the right host. Eventually, the VM running on the destination host will receive the packet after getting de-encapsulated by the VTEP.

Design decisions for multicast mode VXLAN

As I mentioned, we certainly need to take care of physical network prerequirements in multicast mode VXLAN:

- **IGMP snoop** and **IP multicasting** are required in the switch and router throughout the network.
- Ideally, one VXLAN segment to one multicast group is the recommended way to provide optimal multicast forwarding, which also demands an increase in multicast groups if we have large segments. Something which I have seen in cloud environments, wherein VXLAN networks are created on-the-fly and the cloud provider ensures enough multicast IP is available for 1:1 mapping; that way, a packet forwarded to one tenant won't be seen by other tenants.

Hybrid mode packet walk

Hybrid mode VXLAN is recommended for most large environments, primarily because of the simplicity and limited configuration changes that are demanded in the network. Let's have a look at a hybrid mode VXLAN packet walk:

1. **Virtual Machine A** generates **BUM** traffic.
2. **ESXi A** host encapsulates the **L2 header** with **VXLAN header 5001** and will send it to a physical switch.
3. In this case, an encapsulated L2 header will be send it to a multicast group which is defined on the physical switch. I hope it makes more sense now. The physical switch will deliver the packet to destination ESXi host part of that multicast group, in this case, ESXi B, C, D. In addition to that, ESXi A will send a `Locally_Replicate_BIT` set packet to a remote subnet. This packet will be received by a proxy module called**Multicast Tunnel End Point** (**MTEP**). Again, it is a straightforward answer, since there is a replicate locally bit set, MTEP (ESXi host) will replicate the packet locally to one of the ESXi host that are part of same subnet.
4. MTEP will again send the packet to a physical switch and the physical switch will deliver the packet to all the host part of same multicast group.

Design decisions for hybrid mode VXLAN

Hybrid mode VXLAN being one of most widely used replication modes, I believe all of us will be interested to know the key design decisions:

- **IGMP snoop** is required to be configured on a physical switch throughout the VXLAN network.
- IP multicast is not required in the physical router throughout the network. I'm not sure if I'm safe enough to say that, because replication modes can be selected per logical switch, which means we can deploy a logical switch in unicast, multicast, or hybrid mode. What if we are deploying logical switch A in multicast and logical switch B in hybrid mode in the same VXLAN domain? It demands IP multicasting in physical networking. But again, we don't need IP multicasting explicitly for hybrid mode VXLAN networking.

It is strongly recommended to define an **IGMP Querier** for each VLAN to ensure successful L2 multicast delivery and avoid non-deterministic behavior. In order for IGMP, and thus IGMP snooping, to function, a multicast router must exist on the network and generate IGMP queries. The tables created for snooping (holding the member ports for each multicast group) are associated with the querier. I believe we have a strong foundation in VXLAN and its replication modes; let's move on to the connectivity of logical switches and virtual machines.

Connecting virtual machines to logical switches

Since we have already created logical switches, let's go ahead and connect logical switches to the following virtual machines:

- **Two web servers**: web-sv-01a and web-sv-02a
- **One DB server**: DB-sv-01a
- **Application server**: app-sv-01a

Let us see how to connect the logical switches:

1. Click the **vSphere Web Client** home icon.
2. On the **vSphere Web Client** home tab, click **Inventories | Networking & Security**.
3. In the left navigation pane, select **Logical Switches**. In the center pane, select the **App-Tier** logical switch.
4. Click the **Add Virtual Machines** icon, or select **Add VM** from the **Actions** drop-down menu.

5. In the **App-Tier**, add virtual machines dialog box.
6. In the filter list, select the **app-01a** check boxes.
7. Click **Next**. In the **Select VNICs** list, select the **Network Adapter 1 (VM Network)** check box.
8. Click **Next** as shown in the following screenshot:

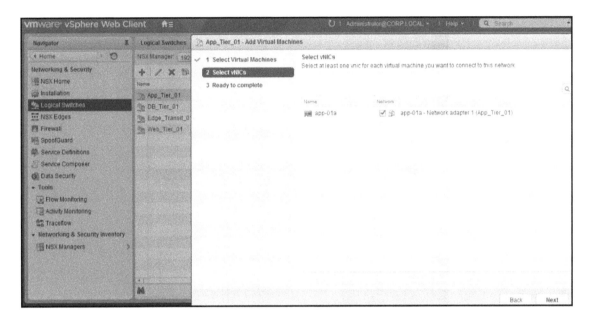

9. Click **Finish**.
10. Repeat Steps 1-7 and connect both the web servers (web-sv-01a, web-sv-02a) and DB server.

Testing connectivity

As we know that our three-tier application, web, app, and DB, is connected to logical switches, let's do some basic testing to confirm their connectivity:

1. Firstly, go ahead and power on those machines.
2. Click the **vSphere Web Client** home icon.
3. On the **vSphere Web Client** home tab, click the **Inventories | VMs and Templates** icon.

4. Expand the VMs and templates inventory tree and power on each of the following virtual machines found in the discovered virtual machine folder:

- web-sv-01a
- web-sv-02a
- app-sv-01a
- db-sv-01a

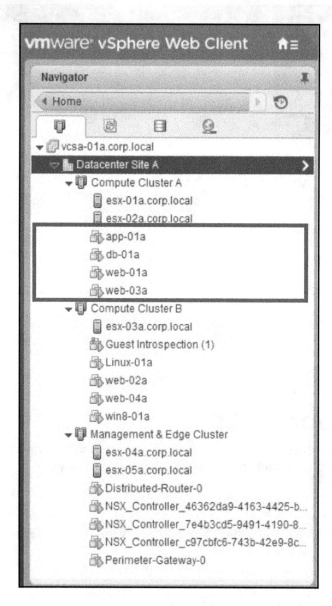

5. To power on a virtual machine, select the virtual machine in the inventory, then select **Power On** from the **Actions** drop-down menu.

6. Once the machines are powered on, we will go ahead and record their IP address:

   - web-01a: 172.16.10.11
   - web-02a: 172.16.10.12
   - app-01a: 172.16.20.11
   - DB-01a: 172.16.30.11

We now do a simple ping test between web-01a and app-01a as shown in the following screenshot:

```
web-sv-01a:~ #
web-sv-01a:~ # ping -c   2 172.16.20.11
PING 172.16.20.11 (172.16.20.11) 56(84) bytes of data.
From 172.16.10.11: icmp_seq=1 Destination Host Unreachable
From 172.16.10.11 icmp_seq=1 Destination Host Unreachable
From 172.16.10.11 icmp_seq=2 Destination Host Unreachable

--- 172.16.20.11 ping statistics ---
2 packets transmitted, 0 received, +3 errors, 100% packet loss, time 1000ms
, pipe 2
web-sv-01a:~ # _
```

Why do we have 100% packet loss when we ping web-01a (172.16.10.11) and app-01a (172.16.20.11)? Will a logical switch perform a Layer 3 routing? Definitely not. The traditional way of performing routing for such networks would be through a physical router, which is nothing but going all the way out of the rack, gets it routed to the right destination. Let's not do that legacy routing in this case, we would leverage NSX logical router capability.

The Distributed Logical Router

The whole purpose of routing is to process the packets between two different IP networks. Let's discuss the fundamentals of routing before getting into logical routers. Every router will build a routing table, which will have information about **destination network, next hop router, metrics, and administrative distance**. There are two methods of building a routing table:

- **Static routing**: Static routing is manually created and updated by a network administrator. Based on the network topology, we will be in need of configuring a static route on each and every router for end-to-end network connectivity. Even though this gives full control over the routing, it would be an extremely tedious job to configure routes on a large network.
- **Dynamic routing**: Dynamic routing is created and updated by a routing protocol running on a router; **Routing Information Protocol (RIP)** and **Open Shortest Path First (OSPF)** are some examples. Dynamic routing protocols are intelligent enough to choose a better path whenever there is a change in routing infrastructure.

The VMware NSX Distributed Logical Router supports static routes, OSPF, ISIS, and BGP routing protocols. It is important to know that dynamic routing protocols are supported only on external interface (uplink) of the **Distributed Logical Router (DLR)**. The DLR allows an ESXi hypervisor to locally do routing intelligence, through which we can optimize East-West data plane traffic.

Deploying a Distributed Logical Router

A DLR is a virtual appliance which has the control plane intelligence and it relies on NSX Controllers to push the routing updates to the ESXi kernel modules.

Procedure for deploying a logical router

Let's walk through the step-by-step configuration of a Distributed Logical Router:

1. In the vSphere web client, navigate to **Home** | **Networking & Security** | **NSX Edges**.

Select the appropriate NSX Manager on which to make your changes. If you are creating a universal logical router, you must select the primary NSX Manager. We will be discussing about Primary/Secondary NSX manager concepts in `Chapter 7`, *NSX Cross vCenter*.

2. Select the type of router you wish to add; in this case, we would add **logical router**.

3. Select **Logical (Distributed) Router** to add a logical router local to the selected NSX Manager.

 Since we haven't discussed the cross-vCenter NSX environment, we won't leverage a universal logical distributed router in this chapter.

4. Type a name for the device. This name appears in your **vCenter inventory**. The name should be unique across all logical routers within a single tenant. Optionally, you can also enter a hostname. This name appears in the CLI. If you do not specify the hostname, the edge ID, which gets created automatically, is displayed in the CLI.

5. The **Deploy Edge Appliance** option is selected by default. An edge appliance (also called a logical router virtual appliance) is required for dynamic routing and the logical router appliance's firewall, which applies to logical router pings, SSH access, and dynamic routing traffic. You can deselect the **Deploy Edge Appliance** option if you require only static routes, and do not want to deploy an edge appliance. You cannot add an edge appliance to the logical router after the logical router has been created.

6. The **Enable High Availability** option is not selected by default. Select the **Enable High Availability** check box to enable and configure high availability. High Availability is required if you are planning to do dynamic routing. I want everyone to think from a cloud provider perspective: if your tenant is requesting the High Availability feature, how do you satisfy that requirement? NSX Edge replicates the configuration of the primary appliance for the standby appliance and ensures that the two HA NSX Edge virtual machines are not on the same ESXi host even after you use DRS and vMotion. Two virtual machines are deployed on vCenter in the same resource pool and data store as the appliance you configured. Local link IPs are assigned to HA virtual machines in the NSX Edge HA so that they can communicate with each other. But remember that instead of one control VM, we have two control VMs running now so definitely it will consume twice the compute resource.

The following screenshot shows NSX DLR-VM deployment:

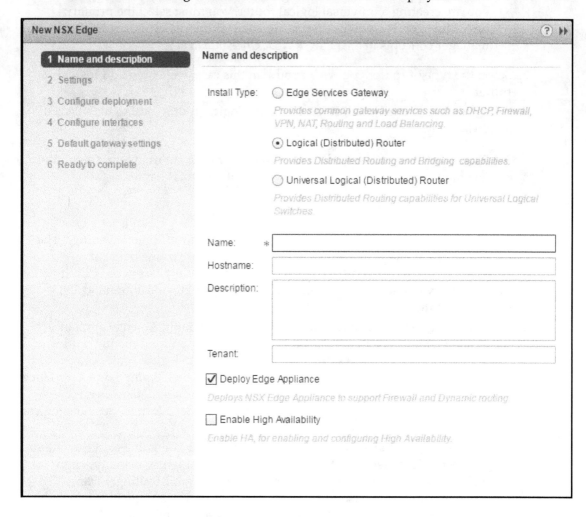

7. Type and retype a password for the logical router. The password must be 12-255 characters and must contain the following:
   - At least one uppercase letter
   - At least one lowercase letter
   - At least one number
   - At least one special character

8. Enable **SSH** and set the log level (optional). By default, **SSH** is disabled. If you do not enable SSH, you can still access the logical router by opening the virtual appliance console. Enabling SSH here causes the SSH process to run on the logical router virtual appliance, but you will also need to adjust the logical router firewall configuration manually to allow SSH access to the logical router's protocol address. The protocol address is configured when you configure dynamic routing on the logical router. By default, the log level is emergency.

 On logical routers, only IPv4 addressing is supported.

9. Configure the interfaces. Under Configure interfaces, add four **logical interfaces** (**LIFs**) to the logical router:
   - Uplink connected to **Transit-Network-01** logical switch with an IP of 192.168.10.2/29
   - Internal connected to **Web-Tier-01 Logical Switch** with IP 172.16.10.1/24
   - Internal connected to **App-Tier-01 Logical Switch** with IP 172.16.20.1/24
   - Internal connected to **DB-Tier-01 Logical Switch** with IP 172.16.30.1/24

The following screenshot depicts the **Add Interface** screen:

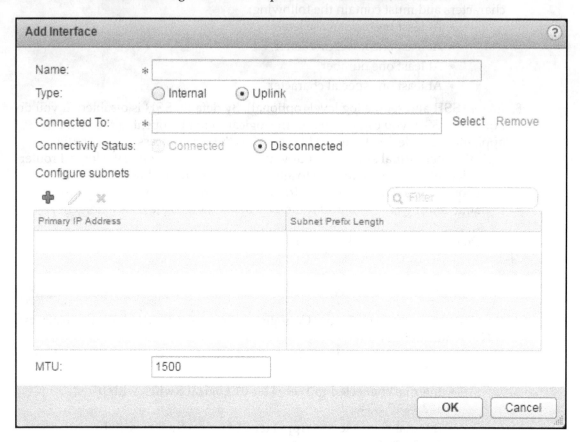

9. Configure interfaces of this NSX Edge: Internal interfaces are for connections to logical switches that allow VM-to-VM (East-West) communication. Internal interfaces are created on the logical router virtual appliance and we call them LIF. Uplink interfaces are for North-South communication. A logical router uplink interface can be connected to an NSX Edge services gateway, third-party router VM, or a VLAN-backed dvPortgroup to make the logical router connection to a physical router directly. You must have at least one uplink interface for dynamic routing to work. Uplink interfaces are created as vNICs on the logical router virtual appliance.

We can add, remove, and modify interfaces after a logical router is deployed.

The following screenshot depicts the DLR configuration that we have performed so far:

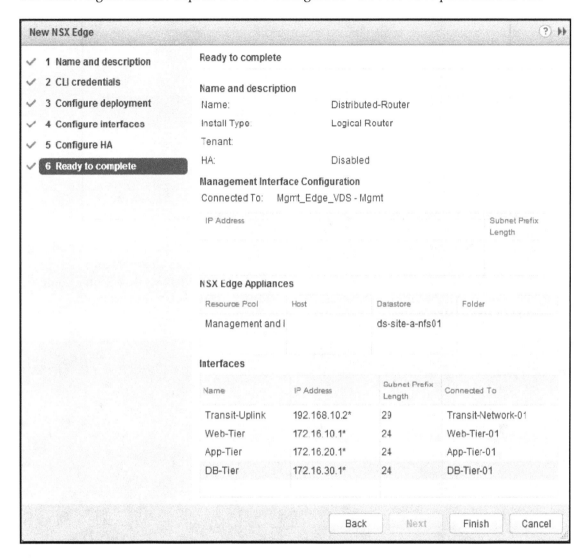

Now that we have successfully deployed a DLR and configured with logical interfaces, we would expect the DLR to perform basic routing functionality for web, app, and DB machines to communicate with each other, which was not possible earlier.

The following screenshot depicts the three-tier application architecture without routing:

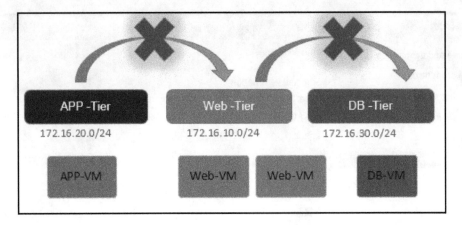

Let's go ahead and perform a quick ping test between `web-01a` (`172.16.10.11`) and `app` (`172.16.20.11`). As we can see from the following screenshot, web servers and application servers are able to communicate each other since we have a Distributer Logical Router, which does the routing in this case. The first ping result is before adding the Distributed Logical Router:

```
web-sv-01a:~ #
web-sv-01a:~ # ping -c  2 172.16.20.11
PING 172.16.20.11 (172.16.20.11) 56(84) bytes of data.
From 172.16.10.11: icmp_seq=1 Destination Host Unreachable
From 172.16.10.11 icmp_seq=1 Destination Host Unreachable
From 172.16.10.11 icmp_seq=2 Destination Host Unreachable

--- 172.16.20.11 ping statistics ---
2 packets transmitted, 0 received, +3 errors, 100% packet loss, time 1000ms
, pipe 2
web-sv-01a:~ #
web-sv-01a:~ # ping -c  2 172.16.20.11
PING 172.16.20.11 (172.16.20.11) 56(84) bytes of data.
64 bytes from 172.16.20.11: icmp_seq=1 ttl=63 time=56.5 ms
64 bytes from 172.16.20.11: icmp_seq=2 ttl=63 time=1.46 ms

--- 172.16.20.11 ping statistics ---
2 packets transmitted, 2 received, 0% packet loss, time 1001ms
rtt min/avg/max/mdev = 1.466/28.993/56.520/27.527 ms
web-sv-01a:~ #
```

So far, we have discussed the **Distributed Logical Router** (**DLR**), which allows ESXi hypervisor to locally do routing intelligence through which we can optimize East-West data plane traffic. But I know we are very keen to view the DLR routing table in an ESXi host. Let's focus on the following screenshot to know the network topology.

The following screenshot depicts the three-tier application architecture with DLR connection:

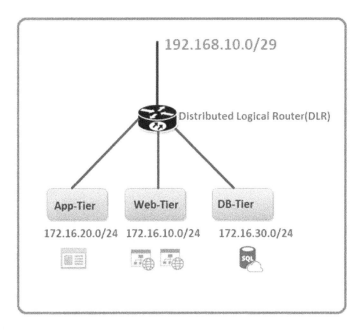

The following questions might come to our mind:

- How many networks do we have?
  - 172.16.10.0/24
  - 172.16.20.0/24
  - 172.16.30.0/24
  - 192.168.10.0/29
- Are the networks directly connected to the router?
  - Yes, they are connected to the router.

We will go ahead and SSH to one of the ESXi hosts to check the logical router instance, MAC, ARP, and routing tables, which will certainly give granular-level details:

```
Net-vdr -I -l
```

The preceding command will display the logical router instance as shown in the following screenshot. You can see the following parameters:

- VDR Name is default+edge-19
- Number of Lifs is 4
- Remember we connected four logical networks to the distributed router? Hence the count is 4
- Number of Routes is 4

Since we have connected four logical networks, the router is aware of those directly connected networks:

```
🖳 esx-01a.corp.local - PuTTY

~ # net-vdr -I -l

VDR Instance Information :
--------------------------

VDR Instance:            default+edge-19:1969527534
Vdr Name:                default+edge-19
Vdr Id:                  1969527534
Number of Lifs:          4
Number of Routes:        4
State:                   Enabled
Controller IP:           192.168.110.202
Control Plane Active:     Yes
Control Plane IP:        192.168.110.51
Edge Active:             No
```

The following command will verify the network routes discovered by DLR:

```
net-vdr --route -l VDR Name
```

For example:

```
net-vdr --route -l default+edge-19
```

The logical router routing table is pushed by the NSX Controller to the ESXi host and it will be consistent across all the ESXi hosts. You will see the following output:

```
~ # net-vdr -l --route default+edge-19

VDR default+edge-19:1969527534 Route Table
Legend: [U: Up], [G: Gateway], [C: Connected], [I: Interface]
Legend: [H: Host], [F: Soft Flush] [!: Reject]

Destination     GenMask         Gateway       Flags   Ref Origin  UpTime  Interface
-----------     -------         -------       -----   --- ------   ------  ---------
172.16.10.0     255.255.255.0   0.0.0.0       UCI     1   MANUAL   5472    75649aee0000000a
172.16.20.0     255.255.255.0   0.0.0.0       UCI     1   MANUAL   5472    75649aee0000000b
172.16.30.0     255.255.255.0   0.0.0.0       UCI     1   MANUAL   5472    75649aee0000000c
192.168.10.0    255.255.255.248 0.0.0.0       UCI     1   MANUAL   5472    75649aee00000002

~ #
```

Now log in to the controller CLI to view the logical router state information:

```
nvp-controller # show control-cluster logical-routers instance all
(List all LR instances)
```

You will see the following output:

```
nvp-controller # show control-cluster logical-routers instance all
LR-Id       LR-Name        Hosts[]          Edge-Connection Service-Controller
1969527534 default+edge-19 192.168.110.52                   192.168.110.202
                           192.168.210.56
                           192.168.210.51
                           192.168.210.52
                           192.168.110.51
                           192.168.210.57

nvp-controller #
```

The other command is:

```
nvp-controller # show control-cluster logical-routers interface-summary
1460487509
```

All four logical switches (VXLAN 5000, 5001, 5002, and 5003, which we have connected to the logical router) are displaying in the following output with their respective interface IP, which would be the default gateway for web, app, and DB machines. Again, the idea here is to showcase the power of NSX CLI commands, which give granular-level information and are extremely useful when troubleshooting:

```
nvp-controller # show control-cluster logical-routers interface-summary 1969527534
Interface                    Type   Id          IP[]
75649aee00000002             vxlan  5003        192.168.10.2/29
75649aee0000000c             vxlan  5002        172.16.30.1/24
75649aee0000000a             vxlan  5000        172.16.10.1/24
75649aee0000000b             vxlan  5001        172.16.20.1/24
nvp-controller #
```

Understanding logical interfaces

I'm pretty sure we now have a good understanding of how distributed routing works in the NSX environment. Again, NSX DLR is not limited between VXLAN networks; we can certainly leverage the routing functionality between VXLAN and VLAN networks. Let's discuss logical interfaces in more detail:

- If the Distributed Logical Router connects to a vSphere distributed switch port group, the interface is called a **VLAN LIF**. VLAN LIFs make use of **Designated Instance** (**DI**) for resolving ARP queries. The NSX Controller randomly selects one of the ESXi hosts as the designated instance to ease the ARP traffic so that any ARP traffic for that subnet will be handled by one of the ESXi hosts and every other ESXi host is also aware of where DI is running.
- If the Distributed Logical Router connects to a logical switch, the interface is called a **VXLAN LIF**.
- A LIF can either be an uplink or internal.
- Multiple LIFs can be configured on one Distributed Logical Router instance.
- An ARP table is maintained for each LIF.
- Each LIF has assigned an IP address representing the default IP gateway for the logical network it connects to and a vMAC address. The IP address is unique for each LIF, whereas the same virtual MAC is assigned to all the defined LIFs.

- We can configure up to 999 interfaces, with a maximum of eight uplinks.
- The routing table can be populated in multiple ways:
  - Directly connected
  - Static routes
  - OSPF
  - BGP
  - Route redistribution

We will discuss dynamic routing and route redistribution during `Chapter 5`, *NSX Edge Services*, which will give us a clear view on how tenants access public networks (North-South connectivity).

Logical router deployment considerations

Distributed Logical Router (DLR) deployment is highly critical in NSX environments. Let's check a few critical decision factors:

- Ensure that controllers are up-and-running before deploying a logical router.
- Don't deploy a logical router during controller deployment. This is not limited to DLR deployments; it applies for all NSX features.
- If a logical router is to be connected to VLAN dvPortgroups, ensure that all hypervisor hosts with a logical router appliance installed can reach each other on UDP port 6999 for logical router VLAN-based ARP proxy to work.
- Logical router interfaces should not be created on two different distributed port groups (dvPortgroups) with the same VLAN ID if the two networks are in the same vSphere distributed switch.
- Starting with VMware NSX for vSphere 6.2, the L2 bridging feature can now participate in distributed logical routing. The VXLAN network to which the bridge instance is connected will be used to connect the routing instance and the bridge instance. This was unsupported in earlier releases.
- DLR interfaces don't support trunking; however, each DLR interface can be connected to NSX Edge sub-interfaces which support trunking. But we are limited with leveraging IP-Sec, L2-VPN, BGP (dynamic routing), DHCP, and DNAT features on sub-interfaces.

- 1,000 logical interfaces are supported on DLR.
- DLR doesn't support **virtual routing and forwarding** (**VRF**). For true network multitenancy, we need to deploy a unique DLR which can be connected to the same or different NSX Edges.
- **Equal Cost Multi Path** (**ECMP**) is supported in DLR; however, state full firewalls are not supported, primarily because of asymmetric routing behavior.

 We will discuss ECMP and asymmetric routing in the next chapter.

- The DLR control VM should not deployed in the compute cluster. If the host fails, both the data plane and control plane will be impacted at the same time if the control VM is also residing on same ESXi host. So the right place to deploy the DLR control VM will be either on the management cluster or if we have a separate vSphere Edge cluster, that is the best option.

Layer 2 bridges

Logical network to physical network access might be required due to multiple reasons in a NSX environment:

- During **Physical to Virtual** (**P2V**) migrations where changing IP addresses is not an option
- Extending virtual services in the logical switch to external devices
- Extending physical network services to virtual machines in logical switches
- Accessing existing physical network and security resources

Since Layer 2 bridging is a NSX Edge Distributed Logical Router functionality, the L2 bridge runs on the same host on which the edge logical router control virtual machine is running. Bridging is entirely done at kernel level, as it was for Distributed Logical Routing. A special dvPort type called a **sink port** is used to steer packets to the bridge. In the following screenshot, we have a VXLAN environment wherein virtual machines in VXLAN network 5006 need to communicate with a physical site, which is in VLAN-100:

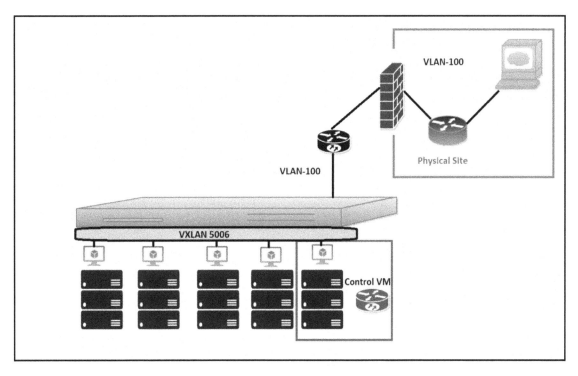

VLAN-100

Physical Site

VLAN-100

VXLAN 5006

Control VM

NSX Layer 2 bridging

Deploying an L2 bridge

Let's have a look at the deployment of a Layer 2 bridge:

1. Log in to the vSphere Web Client.
2. Click **Networking & Security** and then click **NSX Edges**.
3. Double-click a logical router.
4. Click **Manage** and then click **Bridging**.
5. Click the add icon.
6. Type a name for the bridge.
7. Select the logical switch that you want to create a bridge for.
8. Select the distributed virtual port group to which you want to bridge the logical switch.
9. Click **OK**.

In the following example, we are bridging logical switch **bRANCH** with **Mgmt_Edge_VDS** port group which is VLAN enabled:

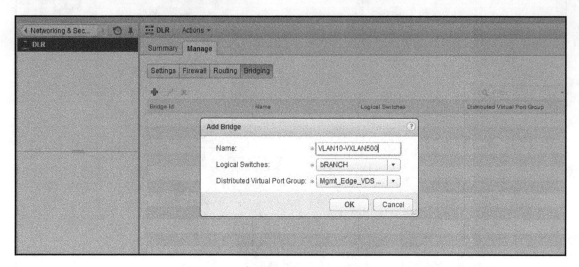

Design considerations for the L2 bridge

Like any other NSX components, L2 bridging is an equally important design decision factor. The following are the key points:

- Bridging VLAN-ID 0 is not supported.
- Multiple bridges are supported per logical router; however, we cannot have more than one bridge instance active per VXLAN-VLAN pair.
- Bridging cannot be used for VLAN-VLAN connection.
- Bridging is not a data center interconnect technology.
- Starting from NSX 6.2, DLR interfaces can be connected to a VXLAN network that is bridged with a VLAN network. Earlier versions don't have this feature.
- Don't mix a DLR and a next hop router (NSX Edge) on the same host; host failure will have a direct impact on both the devices.

- Even though Layer 2 bridging is a great feature, remember that all ARP resolutions are done explicitly by a bridge instance module running on the same host wherein we have deployed the logical router. For the same reason, running too many bridge instances and that too if they all are on the same host in addition to that if we have UTEPs and MTEPs running on the same host there would be certainly a performance impact. So try to run bridge instances on separate hosts as much as we can or, in another words, distribute logical router deployment across the management cluster.

Summary

We started this chapter with an introduction to the NSX Distributed Logical Router and discussed VXLAN replication modes and a few packet walks. Later, we covered a few key design decisions while deploying a DLR. We also discussed the Layer 2 bridging feature of DLRs and we moved on to important design decisions that need to be noted while leveraging bridging functionality.

There are exciting times ahead as we discuss more and more features and their functionalities.

In the next chapter, we will discuss NSX Edge routing and we will establish connectivity with the DLR with a dynamic routing protocol.

5
NSX Edge Services

NSX Edge is a feature rich gateway Virtual Machines which offers L3-L7 services. Edge Gateway is the glue that connects all logical networks provide DHCP, NAT, Routing, VPN, Firewalling, Load Balancing and HA functionality. Ideally these devices will be configured at the perimeter level of vSphere Datacenter.

In this chapter, we will cover the following topics:

- Introducing Edge services
- Introducing Edge service form factors
- Introducing OSPF, BGP, and ISIS protocols
- Routing between DLR and NSX Edge router
- NSX Edge service use cases

Introducing Edge services

NSX Edge gateway is a virtual machine that provides services such as Network Address Translation, Dynamic Host Configuration Protocol, DNS relay, Virtual Private Network, load balancing, and routing functionality. Firstly, there is no rule of thumb that says we should leverage all these features using one single Edge. For true multi-tenancy, we can deploy multiple Edges for different features' use cases. Let's have a look at Edge gateway form factor before we start with routing and other topics.

Introducing Edge form factor

There have been countless times when we would have deployed a virtual machine, assuming some specific value is enough for compute and storage. Later, when we start facing performance issues, we are forced to go back and recheck the application requirements. As far as the impact is concerned, it would be specific to one VM, so going back and forth and making changes is just about feasible. Well, this doesn't work with NSX Edge, primarily because it would be a perimeter device and the impact would be much higher. For the same reason, selecting the right form factor is critical in order to get the best performance. The following screenshot depicts the default compute capacity, which each Edge form factor offers:

Edge Services	vCPU	Memory MB	Use Case
X-Large	6	8192	Suitable for L7 high performance Load Balancer
Quad-Large	4	1024	Suitable for high performance ECMP and Firewall deployment
Large	2	1024	Single Edge Services
Compact	1	512	Small Deployments(POC)

The positive aspect to note is that we can always go back and change these form factors. For example, during initial deployment time, we have deployed NSX Edge in **large form factor**. Later, we can go ahead and change the form factor from **large to any higher version**. However, the negative side is that there will be an NSX Edge service outage during that time. Hence, the recommended deployment option would be selecting the right form factor Edge. For services such as, load balancers, wherein we have a lot of SSL termination and offload tasks, which would consume a lot of vCPU cycles, the preferred form factor would be Edge **X-Large**. With that said, we will start with one of the most exciting topics in the NSX world. Routing simplicity and feature-rich integration makes NSX an ideal platform for all vSphere architects.

Introducing OSP, BGP, and ISIS

As we know, distributed routing capability in the VMware NSX provides an optimized and scalable way of handling East-West traffic in a data center. The NSX Edge services router provides the traditional centralized routing. What more could we need in an enterprise environment? Both these components, **Distributed Logical Router** (DLR) and Edge, give a cutting-edge solution in an enterprise's routing architecture. Before we start with how routing works between these solutions, let me give some quick background on routing protocols that are supported in an NSX environment, and together, we will explore an OSPF routing protocol configuration between DLR and NSX Edge. Sounds interesting? Let's get started.

Exploring Open Shortest Path First

From my experience, while teaching and doing labs, people often find it really difficult to understand the **Open Shortest Path First** (OSPF) protocol. So, let's split this abbreviation into its component parts:

- **Open**: Yes, this is an open standard protocol developed by a wide range of network vendors. This means that it is publicly available on any dynamic routing protocol-supported routers. Again, we are not limited to running OSPF on CISCO or Juniper, or any other vendor routers in an OSPF routing environment. This is certainly configurable in multivendor deployment scenarios.
- **Shortest Path First**: **Shortest Path First** (SPF) uses a Dijkstra algorithm to find the single shortest path to reach a destination network.

So, in a nutshell, we have an open standard routing protocol that calculates the shortest path to reach a destination. For now, we will pause for some time and understand routing classes, and we will come back to the topic of OSPF. There are three classes of routing protocols, as follows:

- **Distance vector**: A distance vector protocol finds the best path to a remote network by judging distance. RIP is a distance vector routing protocol. In RIP routing, to reach the destination network, the router will choose the path that has the least number of hops. The term vector means the direction to the destination network.

- **Link state**: Link state protocols are also called Shortest Path First protocols. In a link state protocol environment, routers create three separate tables:
  - Directly-attached neighbors
  - Topology of the entire network
  - Routing table
  - Behind the scenes, link state protocols send updates containing the state of their own links to all other directly connected routers on the network.
- **Hybrid**: A hybrid protocol is a mix of distance vector and link state protocols, and **Enhanced Interior Gateway Routing Protocol (EIGRP)** is a great example.

Understanding basic OSPF terminology

To understand the fundamentals of OSPF, let's clarify some basic OSPF terminology:

- **Link**: A link is a network, or OSPF router interface, assigned to any given network. Yes, it is important to understand if we have multiple interfaces in an up-and-running state; OSPF wont treat them as link. Only when an interface is added to the OSPF process is it considered to be a link.
- **Router ID**: The **router ID (RID)** is an IP address used to identify the OSPF router.
- **Neighbor**: Neighbors are two or more OSPF routers that have an interface on a common network:
  - Area ID
  - Stub area flag
  - Authentication password
  - Hello and dead intervals

 All the preceding parameters should be matching to form a neighbor ship.

- **Adjacency**: Adjacency is a relationship between two OSPF routers that permits the direct exchange of route updates. This totally depends upon both the type of network and the configuration of the routers:

    - **Designated Router**: A **Designated Router** (**DR**) is elected whenever OSPF routers are connected to the same broadcast network to minimize the number of adjacencies formed. Selection can be either manual or automated, based on priority value as the first pararmeter. All routers on the same network will establish adjacencies with the DR and the BDR, which ensures that all router's topology tables are synchronized.
    - **Backup Designated Router**: A **Backup Designated Router** (**BDR**) is a backupfor the DR router.
    - **Hello protocol**: The OSPF Hello protocol provides dynamic neighbor discovery and maintains neighbor relationships. Hello packets are addressed to multicast address `224.0.0.5`. Hello packets and **Link State Advertisements** (**LSAs**) build the topological database.
    - **Neighborship database**: A neighborship database is a list of all OSPF routers for which Hello packets are visible. Lets discuss about how OSPF database is getting updated.

Updating a topology database

We are aware that the OSPF router teaches **directly attached neighbors**, **topology of the entire internetwork**, and finally, a **routing table**. Let's discuss how a topology database is updated in an OSPF router:

- **Link state advertisement**: I would simply call it an OSPF languageâ◎◎the way OSPF routers communicate. LSA is an OSPF data packet containing link state and routing information that's shared among OSPF routers.

- **Areas**: An OSPF area is a grouping of contiguous networks and routers. All routers in the same area share a common area ID. The following figure depicts a simple OSPF topology:

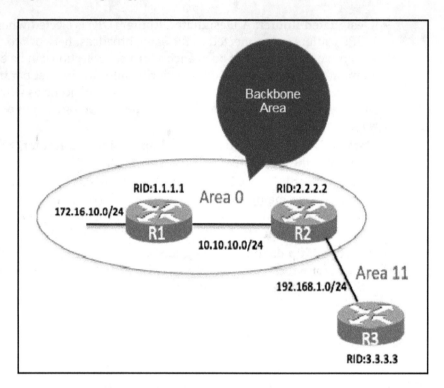

There is a total of eight important LSA types in OSPF:

- **LSA Type 1: Router LSA**: Each router within the area will flood a type 1 router LSA within the area.
- **LSA Type 2: Network LSA**: The network LSA or type 2 is created for each multi-access network. Network LSAs are generated by the designated router.
- **LSA Type 3: Summary LSA: Area Border Router** (ABR) will create a LSA 3 summary and will pass the LSA information to other areas.
- **LSA Type 4: Summary ASBR LSA**: Routers need to know where to find the ASBR. In such cases, ABR will generate a summary.

- **LSA Type 5: Autonomous system external LSA**: A type 5 LSA will be sent by a border router to let other routers know how to reach the border router through the internal network.
- **LSA Type 7: Not-so-stubby area LSA**: This doesn't allow external LSAs (type 5). All it will do is generate type 7 LSAs instead

How about type 6 and type 8? Well, type 6 is no longer supported in OSPF v2 and, type 8 LSA is a link-local only LSA for OSPF v3. A type 8 LSA is used to give information about link-local addresses and a list of IPv6 addresses on the link. In this module, we have a practical use case discussion on OSPF in the NSX world by establishing a dynamic routing between NSX Edge and DLR.

For now, let's move on and discuss ISIS protocol.

Exploring Intermediate System to Intermediate System

An Intermediate System routing protocol is a link state protocol similar to OSPF. It is also called an ISP scale protocol, primarily because of its ability to support more areas than OSPF. An intermediate system is a **router**, and **Intermediate System to Intermediate System (IS-IS)** is the routing protocol that routes packets between intermediate systems. IS-IS routers are of three types: Level 1 (intra area), Level 2 (inter area), or Level 1-2 (both). Routing information is exchanged between Level 1 routers and other Level 1 routers of the same area, and Level 2 routers can only form relationships and exchange information with other Level 2 routers. Level 1-2 routers exchange information with both levels and are used to connect the inter area routers with the intra area routers, as shown in the following screenshot:

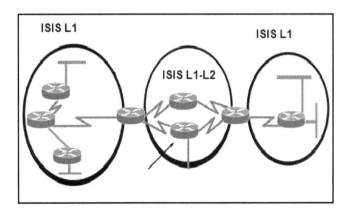

After having a brief glimpse at the ISIS protocol, let us now understand the **Border Gateway Protocol (BGP)**.

Exploring Border Gateway Protocol

First and foremost, this is an exterior gateway protocol. BGP is primarily used by **Internet Service Providers (ISP)** and large enterprise companies when they have connections with multiple ISPs. All it does is bind smaller, autonomous (internetworks) to ensure efficient routing is possible regardless of the location. BGP is basically a group of autonomous systems. This raises another question: what are autonomous systems? **Autonomous Systems (AS)** are groups of networks under a common administration. Just like private and public IP concepts, AS also have private and public numbers. Public AS numbers range from 1 to 64511, and private AS numbers range from 64512 to 65535. When we do a routing within an AS it is called iBGP routing, and eGBP is routing between two different autonomous systems. The process for forming a BGP peering is very simple. A TCP session needs to established, with the BGP source port being an emphemeral port, and the destination being TCP port 179. The following figure depicts a iBGP and eBGP topology:

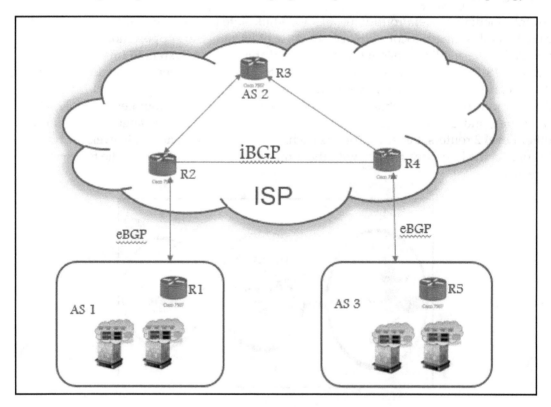

I have limited the explanation of BGP, ISIS, and OSPF, primarily because it would demand writing a different book to cover all aspects of routing protocol. Enough said-let's finish of our network topology by configuring OSPF routing. Before we start with routing between the Distributed Logical Router and the NSX Edge gateway, let's go back to the lab topology that we used in Chapter 4, *NSX Virtual Network and Logical Router*, and understand where we are and what the next requirement is. From the following figure, it is clear that we have established a routing between web, app, and DB networks. It's time to ask a few questions. We need all these networks to communicate with another network (192.168.100.0/24) through a transit network. How do we do that? Can we connect the transit network to NSX Edge and leverage dynamic routing capability so that an app, web, and DB can communicate with external networks?

The following figure depicts a three-tier application leveraging DLR functionality:

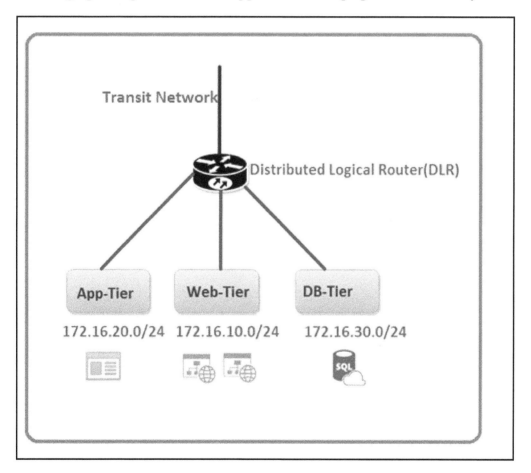

Deploying an NSX Edge gateway

An NSX Edge gateway is a perimeter device and for the same reason, all ingress and egress traffic from a network virtualized data center has to go through Edge devices and finally hit the upstream router. In our case three tier application is in need of communicating with an external network-192.168.100.0/24 which demands an Edge gateway to deployed. Let's deploy an NSX Edge gateway and connect with Distributed Logical Router. In a nutshell, all we are doing is connecting two routers together and creating a dynamic routing environment for them to exchange the networks, so that eventually, our three-tier application can communicate with network 192.168.100.0/24.

The steps are as follows:

1. On the vSphere web client home tab, click **Inventories** | **Networking & Security**.
2. In the left-hand navigation pane, select **NSX Edges**.
3. In the middle pane, click the green plus sign to open the **New NSX Edge** dialog box.
4. On the **Name and description** page, leave **Edge Services Gateway** selected.
5. Enter `Perimeter Gateway` in the **Name** text box and click **Next**.

The following screenshot shows NSX Edge:

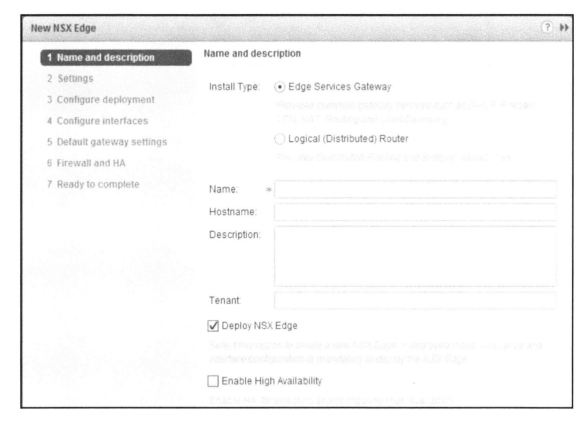

6. On the CLI credentials page, enter the password in the **Password** text box.

7. Enter the password correctly because a verification box is not provided:

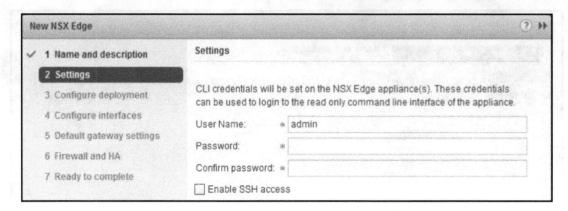

8. On the **Configure deployment** page, verify that the **Datacenter** selection is our Edge Cluster that we created during the initial vSphere Cluster design phase.
9. Verify that the **Appliance Size** selection is **Compact**.
10. Verify that the **Enable auto rule generation** checkbox is selected.

NSX Edge adds firewall, NAT, and routing routes, to enable control traffic to flow for these services. If this option is disabled, we need to manually create firewall rules, which is tedious work.

11. Under **NSX Edge Appliances**, click the green plus sign, as highlighted in the following screenshot, to open the **Add NSX Edge Appliance** dialog box, and perform the following actions:

    1. Select **Management and Edge Cluster** from the **Cluster/Resource Pool** drop-down menu.

    2. Select **shared datastore** from the **Datastore** drop-down menu.

    3. Leave all other fields at the default value and click **OK**.

    4. Click **Next,** as shown in the following sreenshot:

12. On the **Configure interfaces** page, click the green plus sign to open the **Add NSX Edge Interface** dialog box and perform the following actions to configure the first of two interfaces:

1. Enter `Uplink-Interface` in the **Name** text box.
2. For **Type**, leave **UpLink** selected.
3. Click the **Connected To | Select** link.
4. Click **Distributed Portgroup**.
5. Click the **Mgmt-Edge-VDS-HQ Uplink** button and click **OK**.
6. Click the green plus sign under **Configure Subnets**.
7. In the **Add Subnet** dialog box, click the green plus sign to add an IP address field.
8. Enter `192.168.100.3` in the **IP Address** text box and click **OK** to confirm the entry.
9. Enter **24** in the **Subnet prefix length** text box.
10. Click **OK** to close the **Add Subnet** dialog box.
11. Leave all other settings at default value and click **OK**.

13. Click the green plus sign to open the **Add NSX Edge Interface** dialog box, and perform the following actions to configure the second interface:
    1. Enter `Transit-Interface` in the **Name** text box.
    2. For **Type**, click **Internal**.
    3. Click the **Connected To | Select** link.
    4. Click the **Transit-Network** button and click **OK**

The following screenshot shows the NSX Edge Interface selection:

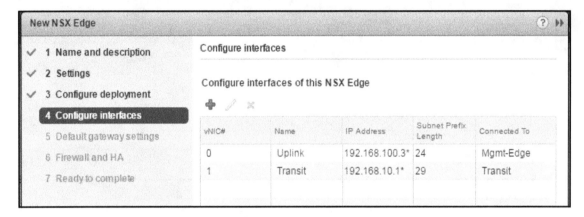

14. Click **Next**.
15. On the **Default gateway settings** page, select the **Configure Default Gateway** check box.
16. Verify that the **vNIC** selection is **Uplink-Interface**.
17. Enter `192.168.100.2` in the **Gateway IP** text box.

18. This value is the IP address of a router that is available on the HQ uplink port group.
19. Leave all the other settings at the default value and click **Next**, as shown in the following screnshot:

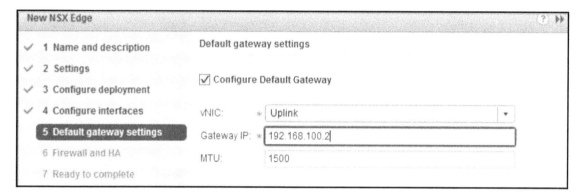

20. On the **Firewall and HA** page, select the **Configure Firewall default policy** check box.
21. For the **Default Traffic Policy**, click **Accept**.

This is a very important step, as you can see that, by default, all traffic is blocked.

Configure HA parameters. High Availability (HA) ensures that an NSX Edge appliance is always available by installing an active pair of Edges on your virtualized infrastructure, which will be discussed further during Edge HA modules. Hence, for the time being, we are leaving the rest of the settings as they are. The following screenshot depicts Edge firewall and HA settings:

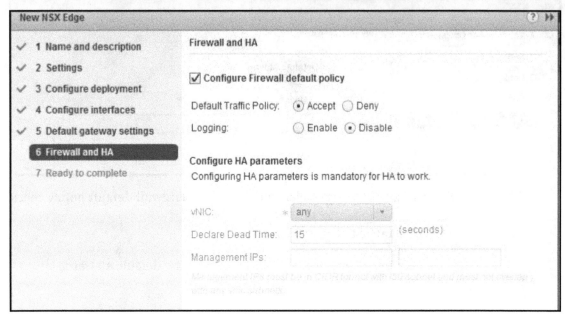

22. On the **Ready to complete page**, review the configuration report and click **Finish**.

So, we have deployed**Distributed Logical Router** and, later, the**NSX Edge gateway**. Once again, the prime aim here is to have our web, app, and DB servers communicating with network 192.168.100.0/24, and we know for sure these networks are not a directly-connected network. Before moving forward with routing, let's have a quick look at the following figure to see our current topology.

The following figure depicts a three-tier application connected to DLR, and a DLR to Edge connection:

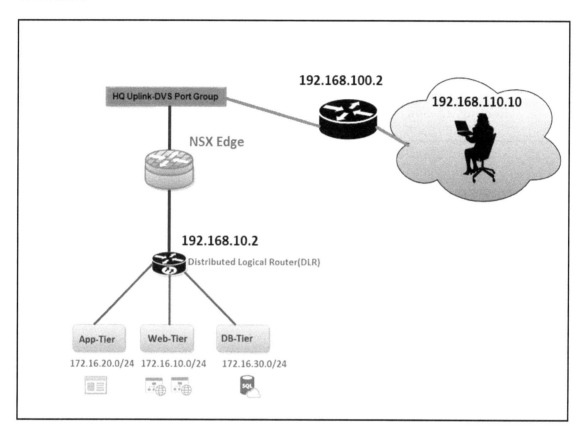

Now that we have completed the NSX Edge deployment, we will go ahead with configuring OSPF on NSX Edge.

Configuring OSPF on NSX Edge

Configuring OSPF routing on NSX Edge (Perimeter Edge) allows logical networks to be learned by the logical router and distributed through a transit network. The steps are as follows:

1. In the routing categories list, select **Global Configuration**.
2. In the **Dynamic Routing Configuration** panel, click **Edit** to open **Edit Dynamic Routing**, as shown in the following screenshot:

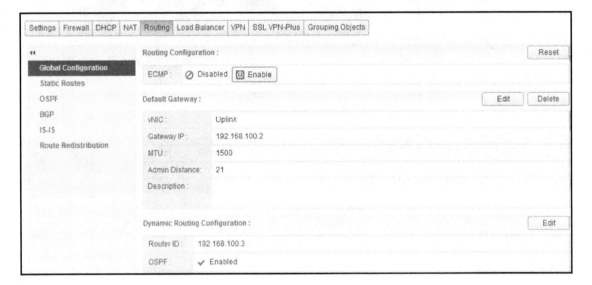

4. In the **Dynamic Routing Configuration** dialog box, perform the following actions:
   - Select **Uplink – 192.168.100.3** from the **Router ID** drop-down menu.
   - Check the **Enable OSPF** checkbox.
   - Leave all other fields at the default value and click **Save**, as shown in the following screenshot:

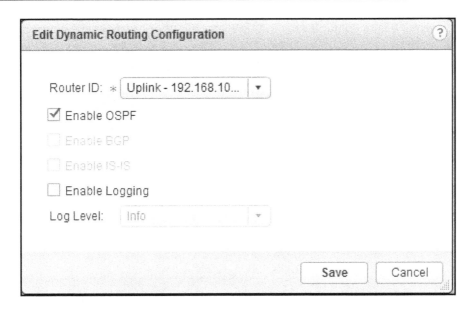

5. At the top of the **Global Configuration** page, click **Publish Changes**.

6. In the routing category panel, select **OSPF**.

7. In the area definitions list, verify that an area with the following properties appears in the list, as shown in the following screenshot:

   - **Area ID**:
   - **Type**: **Normal**
   - **Authentication**: **None**

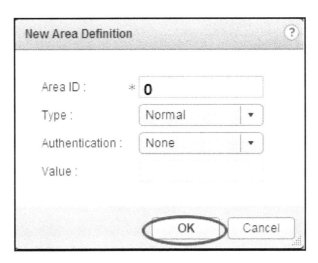

Area 0 is the default area in OSPF and all other areas will be connected to Area 0.

8. Above the area definitions list, click the green plus sign to open the **New Area Definition** dialog box, and perform the following actions:

    - Enter **10** in the **Area ID** text box.

    - Leave all other settings at the default value and click **OK**.

9. Under **Area Interface Mapping**, at the bottom of the **OSPF** page, click the green plus sign to open the **New Area to Interface Mapping** dialog box, and perform the following actions:

    - Verify that the **vNIC** selection is **Uplink-Interface**.

    - Select from the **Area** drop-down menu.

    - Leave all other fields at the default value and click **OK**.

10. Under **Area Interface Mapping**, at the bottom of the **OSPF** page, click the green plus sign to open the **New Area to Interface Mapping** dialog box, and perform the following actions, as shown in the following screenshot:

    - Select **Transit**-Interface from the drop-down menu.

    - Select **10** from the **Area** drop-down menu.

    - Leave all other fields at the default value and click **OK**:

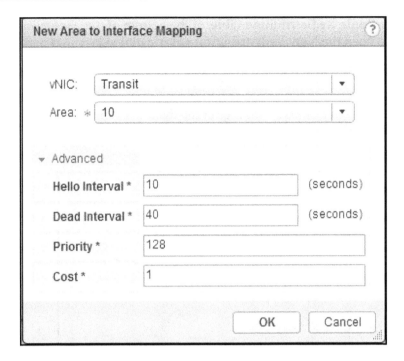

11. At the top of the OSPF page, click **Publish Changes**.

We can configure the type of subnets that are advertised by Perimeter Gateway through OSPF.

12. In the **Routing** category panel, select **Route Redistribution Status**.

13. Under **Route Redistribution table**, at the bottom of the page, click the green plus sign to open the N**ew Redistribution criteria** dialog box, and perform the following actions:
    - Under **Allow learning from**, select the **Connected** checkbox.
    - Subnets connected to Perimeter Gateway can now be learned.
    - Leave all other settings at the default value and click **OK**, as shown in the following screenshot:

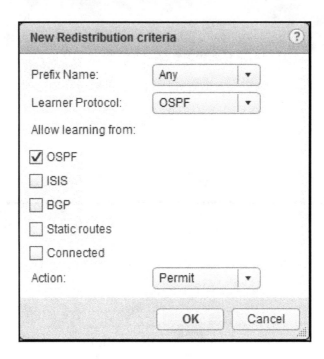

14. In the **Route Redistribution Status** panel, at the top of the page, determine if a green check mark appears next to OSPF. For now, it is not, as shown in the following screenshot:

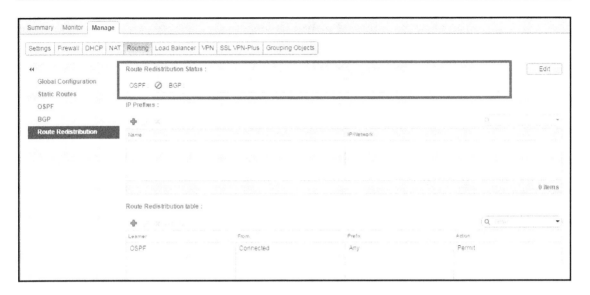

15. If a green check mark does not appear, perform the following actions:

  • On the right-hand side of the **Route Redistribution Status** panel, click **Change**.

  • In the **Change redistribution settings** dialog box, select the **OSPF** checkbox, as shown in the following screenshot:

  • Click **Save**.

  • In the **Route Redistribution Status** panel, at the top of the page, verify that a green check mark appears next to **OSPF**:

16. At the top of the page, click **Publish Changes**:

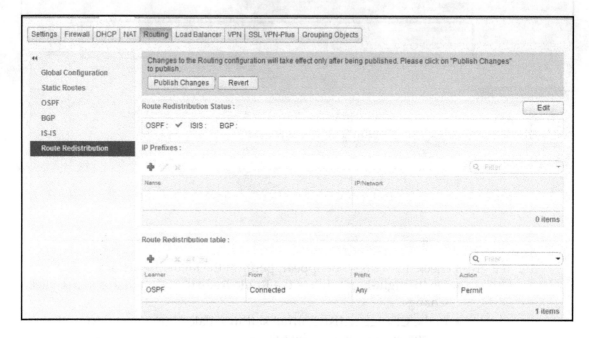

With the preceding steps, we have successfully configured OSPF on Perimeter Edge. All we have done so far is select a **Router-ID** for Perimeter Gateway and enable OSPF. Later, we created Area-10 and performed an Area-to-interface mapping, and finished by enabling **Route Redistribution**. It's time to recollect the firewall policy that we selected during NSX Edge deployment; we have allowed the traffic and also selected the **Enable auto rule generation** checkbox. In this example, we have configured OSPF on NSX Edge and we would expect OSPF auto rules to be configured in the firewall table. Let's verify that by switching to the **Perimeter Gateway | Manage | Firewall** tab, as shown in the following screenshot:

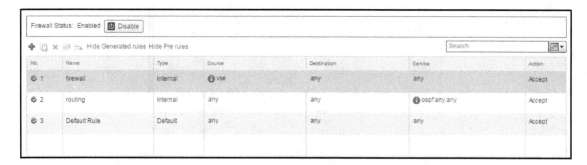

As we can see, there are three firewall rules auto-configured: two **Internal** rules and one **Default** rule. Now that we have an OSPF process running on the NSX Edge and firewall rules are auto-configured, let's move forward and configure OSPF on Distributed Logical Router.

Configuring OSPF routing on Distributed Logical Router

Let me re-emphasize the Distributed Logical Router use case. The whole purpose of DLR is to do an intelligent East-West routing, which allows virtual machine to virtual machine communication without going through traditional data center hop-by-hop routing. Let's go ahead and configure OSPF on DLR:

1. In the **Routing** category panel, select **Global Configuration**.
2. On the right-hand side of the **Dynamic Routing Configuration** panel, click **Edit.**
3. In the **Edit Dynamic Routing Configuration** dialog box, select Interface as **Transit and 192.168.10.2** from the **Router ID** drop-down menu, as shown in the following screenshot:

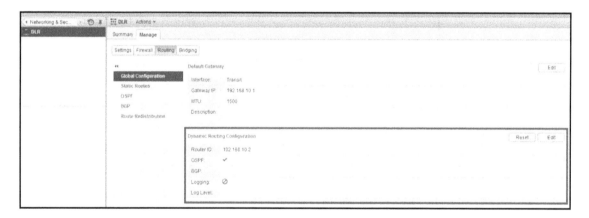

4. This setting must be specified before OSPF can be configured.
5. Leave all other fields at the default value and click **Save**.
6. At the top of the **Global Configuration** page, click **Publish Changes**.
7. In the **Routing** category panel, select **OSPF**.

8. On the right-hand side of the **OSPF Configuration** panel, click **Edit** to open the **OSPF Configuration** dialog box, and perform the following actions:
    1. Select the **Enable OSPF** checkbox.
    2. Enter 192.168.10.3 in the **Protocol Address** text box.
    3. Enter 192.168.10.2 in the **Forwarding Address** text box.

> **Protocol Address**: Establishing routing protocol sessions with other routers. In our example, this address would be used for establishing a routing protocol session with the NSX Edge Perimeter Gateway.
> **Forwarding Address**: IP address that is to be used by the router data path module in the hosts to forward data path packets.

9. Click **OK**:

10. In the **Area Definitions** panel, click the green plus sign to open the **New Area Definition** dialog box.
11. Enter **10** in the **Area ID** text box.
12. Leave all other fields at the default value and click **OK**.
13. In the **Area to Interface Mapping** panel, click the green plus sign to open the **New Area to Interface Mapping** dialog box.
14. Verify that the **Interface** selection is **Transit**.
15. Select **10** from the **Area** drop-down menu.

16. Leave all other fields at the default value and click **OK**.

17. At the top of the **OSPF configuration** page, click **Publish Changes**.

18. After the changes have been published, verify that the **OSPF Configuration Status** is **Enabled**, as shown in the following screenshot:

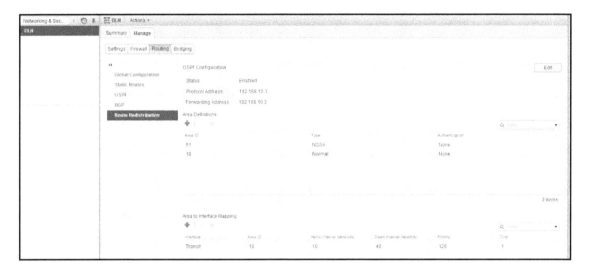

19. We can configure the type of subnets that are advertised by the distributed router, through OSPF:
    - In the **Routing** category panel, select **Route Redistribution**.
    - In the **Route Redistribution table**, select the single entry that appears, click the pencil icon to open the **Edit Redistribution criteria** dialog box, and verify the following settings:
        - **Prefix Name**: Any
        - **Learner Protocol**: OSPF
        - **Allow Learning From**: Connected
        - **Action**: Permit

20. Click **Cancel**.

21. If the default route redistribution entry does not appear in the list or is not configured as specified, create a new route redistribution by clicking the green plus sign and configuring the criteria as specified in Step 13. The following screenshot shows an OSPF route redistribution table:

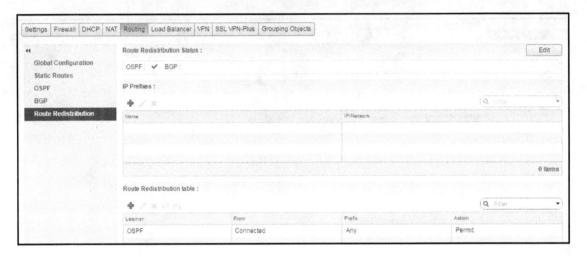

Let's verify the distributed router firewall policy to confirm if we have required rules for OSPF learning. We certainly have OSPF auto rule populated; however, the only difference is that the default rule is **Deny,** as shown in the following screenshot. We will certainly check if that rule is blocking any traffic in our example. For now, we are not changing that rule:

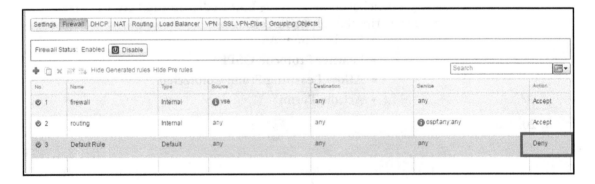

Even though the NSX GUI is nice and cool, there is no way we can view the routing table; we are limited to running CLI commands to check, and we have two methods to do that:

- Direct console to NSX Edge and logical router
- SSH session to NSX Edge and logical router.

Let's SSH to NSX Edge. We are connecting to NSX edge with the IP address 192.168.100.3. There are a few interesting things to note from this output, as shown in the following screenshot:

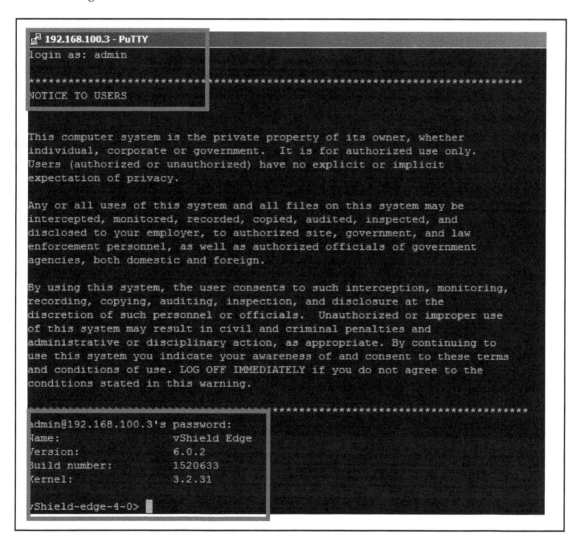

The name is mentioned as **vShield Edge**. Let's not get embarrassed with that output. As explained in `Chapter 1`, *Introduction to Network Virtualization*, NSX is a product that is created from VMware **vCloud Networking Security** (**vCNS**). Irrespective we are doing a greenfield deployment of NSX, or a brownfield deployment where older VCNS was upgraded to NSX, edges would still show as vShield Edge. However, the version would certainly be different based on the VCNS/NSX management version. Let's list a few display commands and make a note of a few configurations:

- `Show IP OSPF interface`: This command would display the interfaces where the OSPF process is running. For example, if a router has 10 interfaces and out of that only two interfaces are connected to OSPF AREA, only those interfaces would be listed:

```
vShield-edge-4-0> show ip ospf interface
vNic_1 is activated
  Internet Address 192.168.10.1, Network Mask 255.255.255.248, Area 0.0.0.10
  Transmit Delay is 1 sec, Network Type BROADCAST, State BDR, Priority 128
  Designated Router's Interface Address 192.168.10.3
  Backup Designated Router's Interface Address 192.168.10.1
  Timer intervals configured, Hello 10, Dead 40, Retransmit 5
vNic_0 is activated
  Internet Address 192.168.100.3, Network Mask 255.255.255.0, Area 0.0.0.0
  Transmit Delay is 1 sec, Network Type BROADCAST, State DR, Priority 128
  Designated Router's Interface Address 192.168.100.3
  Backup Designated Router's Interface Address 0.0.0.0
  Timer intervals configured, Hello 10, Dead 40, Retransmit 5
```

We have two interfaces in our OSPF configuration:

192.168.10.1 (Transit Interface)

192.168.100.3 (Uplink)

- `Show IP OSPF neighbor`: This command shows the IP address of our OSPF neighbor, as shown in the following screenshot of the output:

```
vShield-edge-4-0> show ip ospf neighbor
Neigbhor ID          Priority    Address                   Dead Time    State
192.168.10.2          128        192.168.10.3              30           Full
vShield-edge-4-0>
```

The neighbor ID is `192.168.10.2`. The transit interface (`192.168.10.1`) of NSX Edge is connected to a neighbor DLR, whose IP address is `192.168.10.2`, and their OSPF state is `Full` (in this state, both NSX Edge and DLR are fully adjacent with each other). When OSPF adjacency is formed, a router goes through several state changes before it becomes fully adjacent with its neighbor. The states are `Down`, `Attempt`, `Init`, `2-Way`, `Exstart`, `Exchange`, `Loading`, and `Full`. It took me lot of practice sessions to understand the basics of OSPF. I have done numerous sessions using GNS3, and did a lot of Wireshark capture, which gives a precise picture of how communication is happening and in-depth information on LSA packets. To those of you who are finding it difficult to follow my steps, my request would be to make a note of all these steps and keep drawing the topology.

- `Show IP route`: Show IP route will display the full routing table for that router:

```
vShield-edge-4-0> show ip route

Codes: O - OSPF derived, i - IS-IS derived, B - BGP derived,
C - connected, S - static, L1 - IS-IS level-1, L2 - IS-IS level-2,
IA - OSPF inter area, E1 - OSPF external type 1, E2 - OSPF external type 2

Total number of routes: 8

S       0.0.0.0/0            [1]         via 192.168.100.2
O   E2  172.16.10.0/24       [1]         via 192.168.10.2
O   E2  172.16.20.0/24       [1]         via 192.168.10.2
O   E2  172.16.30.0/24       [1]         via 192.168.10.2
C       192.168.10.0/29      [0]         via 192.168.10.1
C       192.168.10.1/32      [0]         via 0.0.0.0
C       192.168.100.0/24     [0]         via 192.168.100.3
C       192.168.100.3/32     [0]         via 0.0.0.0
```

From the preceding screenshot, we see that:

A total of eight routes are populated and out of that, we have three OSPF routes for networks 172.16.10.0, 172.16.20.0, and 172.16.30.0/24

Have a look at the yellow highlighted column to know through which IP address NSX Edge perimeter gateway is learning it- 192.168.10.2(DLR Transit Interface)

- `Show IP OSPF database`: This command shows the IPv4 OSPF database. The worst way to troubleshoot an OSPF would be by not looking at the database. The fundamental problem I have seen is that we find the output very lengthy and we are unsure where to start and what to look at. Have a look at the following OSPF database output, which we have captured from NSX Edge. Even in a simple network, the topology table looks very lengthy and confusing, just assume an enterprise network OSPF database? The following screenshot depicts an OSPF database:

```
192.168.100.3 - PuTTY
vShield-edge-4-0> show ip ospf database

                Router Link States (Area   0.0.0.0)

Link ID           ADV Router        Age        Seq Num        Checksum
192.168.100.3     192.168.100.3     1531       0x80000003     0x0000f6e6

                Summary Network Link States (Area   0.0.0.0)

Link ID           ADV Router        Age        Seq Num        Checksum
192.168.10.0      192.168.100.3     1526       0x80000003     0x00004ad2

                Summary ASB Link States (Area   0.0.0.0)

Link ID           ADV Router        Age        Seq Num        Checksum
192.168.10.2      192.168.100.3     1520       0x80000003     0x000052c0

                Opaque Area Link States (Area   0.0.0.0)

Link ID           ADV Router        Age        Seq Num        Checksum
1.0.0.1           192.168.100.3     1575       0x80000003     0x00005d4e
1.0.0.2           192.168.100.3     1531       0x80000003     0x00008b46
1.0.0.3           192.168.100.3     1531       0x80000003     0x00000a7c

                Router Link States (Area   0.0.0.10)

Link ID           ADV Router        Age        Seq Num        Checksum
192.168.10.2      192.168.10.2      1528       0x80000004     0x00001b5b
192.168.100.3     192.168.100.3     1531       0x80000003     0x00009928

                Network Link States (Area   0.0.0.10)

Link ID           ADV Router        Age        Seq Num        Checksum
192.168.10.3      192.168.10.2      1533       0x80000003     0x0000b577

                Summary Network Link States (Area   0.0.0.10)

Link ID           ADV Router        Age        Seq Num        Checksum
192.168.100.0     192.168.100.3     1526       0x80000003     0x00009229

                Opaque Area Link States (Area   0.0.0.10)

Link ID           ADV Router        Age        Seq Num        Checksum
1.0.0.1           192.168.10.2      1075       0x80000004     0x0000acb3
1.0.0.1           192.168.100.3     1575       0x80000003     0x00005d4e
1.0.0.2           192.168.10.2      1030       0x80000004     0x000037a7
1.0.0.2           192.168.100.3     1531       0x80000003     0x00008b46
1.0.0.3           192.168.100.3     1531       0x80000003     0x00000a7c
```

For now, we will make a note of a few configuration details:

- OSPF is a link state routing protocol. Based on the types of Network and Area, it will have a unique Link State table. Hence, we are seeing the same in the output.
- In our example, we have two Areas:
  - Link ID – This is the OSPF router ID for L1 and type L2. However, for L3, an L5 type LSA, link ID is a network address.
  - Types of link state for Area-10:
    - Router link state
    - Network link state
    - Summary link state
    - Opaque area link state
  - Area 0 (backbone area)
  - Area 10 (normal area we created)

Here's another brain twisting question: Why do we have Network Link State LSA for Area 10? All we have done is connect a DLR OSPF router to NSX Edge through a transit network, which is a point-to-point connection. Well, this is where I need more focus from everyone. Transit-Network is a logical switch, which is nothing but a vSphere PortGroup (L2 segment). This is the prime reason we have a network LSA in Area 10. Routers are not connected as point-to-point; rather, they are connected to one logical switch and **Designated Router** (**DR**) will send the type 2 LSA. In summary LSA will help the router reach the prefix from one area to another area. Opaque LSA is used in practical applications on a routing platform (MPLS traffic engineering).

Enough talk-the whole purpose of explaining this picture is that ideally, when the OSPF routing tables are populated, we end up by doing a simple ping test and we never think about how they actually work. There is lot more we can discuss about OSPF; however, it is really out of the scope of this book. Let's take a look at the following diagram, which showcases the entire topology with the OSPF routing table:

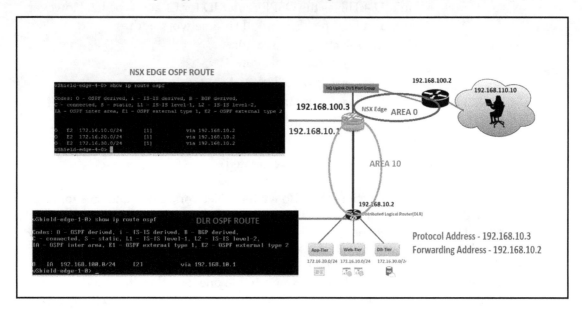

With dynamic routing capability between DLR and NSX Edge, our three-tier applications should be able to reach the `192.168.110.10` machine and vice versa. Let's log in to the application server and confirm if we can reach `192.168.110.10`.

The following screenshot shows successful connectivity from the application server (172.16.20.11) to external network 192.168.110.0/24, which was not possible earlier:

```
172.16.20.11 - PuTTY                                            _ □ ×
          inet addr:172.16.20.11  Bcast:172.16.20.255  Mask:255.255.255.0
          UP BROADCAST RUNNING MULTICAST  MTU:1500  Metric:1
          RX packets:61 errors:0 dropped:0 overruns:0 frame:0
          TX packets:59 errors:0 dropped:0 overruns:0 carrier:0
          collisions:0 txqueuelen:1000
          RX bytes:8760 (8.5 Kb)  TX bytes:10368 (10.1 Kb)

lo        Link encap:Local Loopback
          inet addr:127.0.0.1  Mask:255.0.0.0
          UP LOOPBACK RUNNING  MTU:16436  Metric:1
          RX packets:10 errors:0 dropped:0 overruns:0 frame:0
          TX packets:10 errors:0 dropped:0 overruns:0 carrier:0
          collisions:0 txqueuelen:0
          RX bytes:796 (796.0 b)  TX bytes:796 (796.0 b)

app-sv-01a:~ # ping -c 2 192.168.110.10
PING 192.168.110.10 (192.168.110.10) 56(84) bytes of data.
64 bytes from 192.168.110.10: icmp_seq=1 ttl=125 time=2.77 ms
64 bytes from 192.168.110.10: icmp_seq=2 ttl=125 time=2.37 ms

--- 192.168.110.10 ping statistics ---
2 packets transmitted, 2 received, 0% packet loss, time 1001ms
rtt min/avg/max/mdev = 2.370/2.573/2.776/0.203 ms
app-sv-01a:~ #
```

That concludes our routing module. I know it is hard to recollect all we did so far to establish a virtualized routing environment. I would summarize it in six steps to make it easy to remember:

1. Created three logical switches.
2. Deployed a distributed logical router from the NSX Manager.
3. NSX Controller pushed the DLR configuration to underlying ESXi host.
4. Deployed an NSX Edge device and configuring OSPF on Edge and DLR.
5. All learned routes get pushed to NSX Controller.
6. NSX Controller updates the ESXi host DLR routing table.

We will now move on to the next sections.

NSX routing design decisions

Assume that we have already decided what routing protocol is required for a particular use case. Design factors are key in ensuring that they work flawlessly:

- If we are a service provider, and multi tenancy is required for DLR control VM and **Edge Services Gateway (ESG)**, we should deploy a separate instance, which would ease the management. We can also achieve true isolation between the tenants.
- **Area Border Router (ABR)** should be a physical router.
- If we are not leveraging the **High Availability (HA)** feature for ESG and DLR, ensure that tenant ESG and DLR VM are not residing on the same ESXi host. However, recommended practice would be to leverage HA for DLR control VM and ESG with vSphere HA.
- If there is a shortage of interfaces in ESG, we should leverage the trunk interface so that multiple DLR can be connected to the same ESG.
- DLR to DLR peering is not possible.
- **IPsec** with dynamic routing is not supported.
- Use route summarization wherever we can.
- DLR control VM doesn't support ABR configuration; however, it supports normal and NSSA areas.

Based on the type of physical network and vendors that we choose, there are a lot of other design parameters, which we need to follow explicitly to ensure we are getting the best of both worlds. I would highly recommend reading vendor design guides before implementing NSX. I don't expect everyone to do a Google search. In the Chapter 8, *NSX Troubleshooting*, I will provide all external guide links, to which we should refer before deploying an NSX setup.

NSX Edge NAT

How do we merge two intranets with duplicate addresses and ensure that the host assigned with a private IP can communicate with other hosts through the Internet? There is only one solution for it: **Network Address Translation (NAT)**.

NSX Edge NAT supports two types of NAT services:

- **Source NAT (SNAT)**: Translates the internal private IP address to a public address for outbound access
- **Destination NAT (DNAT)**: Translates the public IP address to an internal private address for inbound access

Okay, let's have a look at how this whole feature works. In the following figure, one of our application servers is in need of communicating with the public network. We can see the application server **172.16.20.1** sending an outbound packet to NSX Edge. Based on the NAT entries, which the NSX administrator would have configured earlier, Edge will perform a NAT table lookup. Since we have a **Source NAT**, which is configured for **172.16.20.1**, it will translate the IP to **170.168.2.1**, which is the public IP. This is a very simple example of 1:1 NAT configuration for outbound access. But remember, Edge also has a firewall feature, and by default, it will block all traffic. So, doing a NAT alone won't do the trick; we need to allow respective source and destination IP in the firewall table:

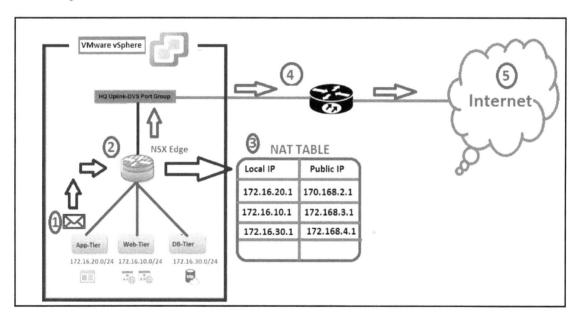

Now let's go ahead and check how a NAT table configuration looks in NSX Edge:

1. Log into VMware vSphere web client and switch to the **Networking & Security** solution page.
2. On the **NSX Edge management** page, double-click the NSX Edge instance that handles the NAT. The following screenshot shows the NSX Edge NAT configuration:

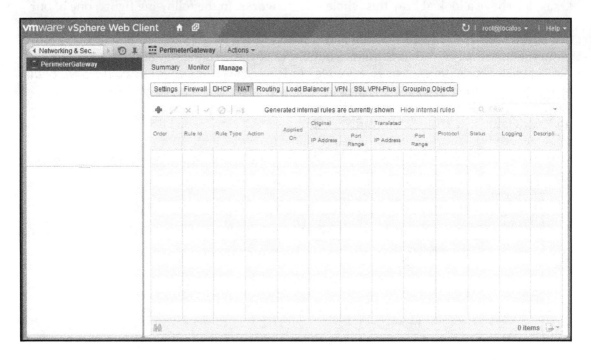

Since we don't have any rule created, as of now, nothing is populated there. Let's explore DNAT and SNAT options further:

Click the add icon, select **Add DNAT Rule**, and configure the following settings based on the business use case:

- **Applied On**: The interface on which to apply the destination NAT rule, for example, external link. The drop-down menu will display the names of all 10 interfaces of this NSX Edge instance.

- **Orginal IP**: The original (public) IP address in one of the following formats:
  - IP address 172.168.2.1
  - IP address range172.168.2.1-172.168.2.3
  - IP address/Subnet 172.168.2.1/24
- **Protocol**: The protocols that are used by the application (we could simply update as A**ny)**
- **Original Port/Range**: The original port, a range of ports, or **Any** port
- **Translated IP/Range**: Since this is a DNAT rule, the translated IP would be the internal/private IP range
- **Translated Port/Range**: The translated port or range of ports in the internal/private network

If all the preceding parameters are configured properly, with firewall rules enabled for the same configuration, our internal machines would be accessible from the public network.In our example we have a done a 1:1 DNAT configuration. This is shown in the following screenshot:

The NAT is an integral part of NSX load balancer functionality, and we need that basic understanding of how NAT works to understand the feature. Last but not least, we are living in a world where nothing is perfect; when something goes wrong, we need to start troubleshooting it. One of the common problems I have seen is not an issue of wrong NAT configuration, it is the intermediate culprit, firewall, which blocks all the traffic, and one would simply wonder, *What the heck am I missing in this setup?* Okay, enough talk. Let's move on and discuss NSX Edge logical load balancer.

NSX Edge logical load balancer

When we talk about load balancers, traditional load balancers are typically placed in the aggregation layer. Load balancing can be implemented with hardware, software, or a combination of both. One of the first methods of load balancing was round-robin DNS. In the current cloud era, we have applications running in multitenant environments and the number of load balancer requirements also gets increased. In a nutshell, if every application tier needs a load balancer, it is extremely difficult to get an optimal performance. This is where virtual load balancers are really making a difference, compared with physical load balancers.

The NSX Edge load balancer enables network traffic to follow multiple paths to a specific destination. A load balancer distributes incoming service requests evenly among multiple servers (virtual machines). Load balancing thus helps to achieve optimal resource use, maximizing throughput, minimizing response time, and avoiding overload. NSX Edge provides load balancing up to Layer 7. Let's get familiarized with some load balancer terms and terminology that is very common in all load balancers.

Server pools

Groups of machines that are running similar applications get added to this pool. This is one of the key design decisions to plan while deploying a load balancer. Firstly, identify the set of virtual machines that are required to be in the server pool.

Virtual server

This is the address from which server pool machines will receive sessions from the load balancer. Each virtual server will have a unique **Virtual IP** (**vIP**). The vIP is an IP address and also contains the service port number.

Application profile

The application profile is where we would configure what type of access protocol (TCP, HTTP, and HTTPS) is used and what type of load balancing algorithm we should use. NSX load balancer supports a wide range of load balancing algorithms.

NSX load balancer operates in two modes:

- **Proxy mode**: The one-arm load balancer mode is also called proxy mode. The NSX Edge gateway uses one interface to advertise the vIP address and to connect to the web servers.
- **Inline mode**: Inline load balancer mode is also called transparent mode. The NSX Edge gateway uses the following interfaces:
    - An interface to advertise the vIP address
    - An interface to connect to the web servers
    - Web servers must point to the NSX Edge gateway as the default gateway

Design considerations while load balancing

Several best practices should be followed when setting up an NSX load balancer. Let's read the following points carefully before doing a lab exercise:

- Based on the number of server pools, load balancer numbers will also get increased. However, that way, since each tenant has its own load balancer, management and configuration changes will have no impact on other tenants' load balancers.
- Deploy load balancers in HA mode for High Availability.

- Ensure you don't deploy a load balancer on the same machine where the underlying load-balanced machines are running. Follow the best practice of deploying on a different ESXi host or in a separate management edge cluster.
- Select the right load balancing protocol based on application characteristics. For example, round robin, least connected, hashing, and least loaded are some of the common algorithms.
- One common question is, *do we need an end-to-end SSL connection, or do we need to terminate or offload SSL traffic?*
- Watch out for bandwidth and number of **connections per second** (**CPS**) that the load balancer is capable of.
- A rule of thumb is to test the load balancer functionality before hitting production, especially if this is the first time we are load balancing an application request in an NSX world.
- Lastly, we need to decide whether we are perfectly okay with having too many eggs in one basket. How does that relate to an NSX load balancer? Well, remember that nothing is stopping us configuring routing/NAT/VPN/DHCP and other Edge/DLR services features on the same Edge/DLR. So, carefully plan what type of services are required to run on Edge/DLR.

It's time to recollect all that we have discussed so far in relation to NSX load balancers, and now we have an objective to perform an SSL load balancing against our web servers. However, in this lab, I'm not leveraging SSL certificates for web servers; hence, we will stick with client to load balancer SSL configuration. So let's get started. First and foremost, we don't have any SSL certificate generated so far. In this example, we will use a self-signed certificate and will leverage the same.

Generating a certificate

We will generate a certificate request and instruct the VMware NSX Edge instance to create a self-signed certificate from that request:

1. In the left-hand navigation pane, select **NSX Edges**.
2. In the edge list, double-click the **Perimeter Gateway** entry to manage that object.
3. Click the **Manage** tab and click **Settings**.
4. In the settings category panel, select **Certificates**.

5. Select **Generate CSR** from the **Actions** drop-down menu to open the **Generate CSR** dialog box, and perform the following actions:

- Enter **Webload** in the **Common Name** text box.
- Enter **Loadbalancer** in the **Organization Name** text box.
- Verify that **RSA** is the selected **Message Algorithm**.
- Verify that **2048** is the selected **Key Size**.
- Leave all other settings at the default value and click **OK**.

6. In the certificate list, select the newly generated signing request and select **Self Sign Certificate** from the **Actions** drop-down menu.

7. When prompted, enter **365** in the **Number of days** text box, and click **OK**.

The following screenshot depicts the **Generate CSR** screen where we need to update all the steps that we have discussed so far:

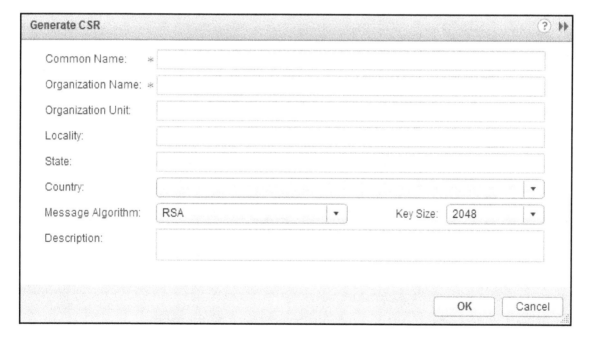

Now that we have a certificate created, we will go ahead and self sign the certificate and use it in our load balancer configuration. The following screenshot depicts the self signed certificate step:

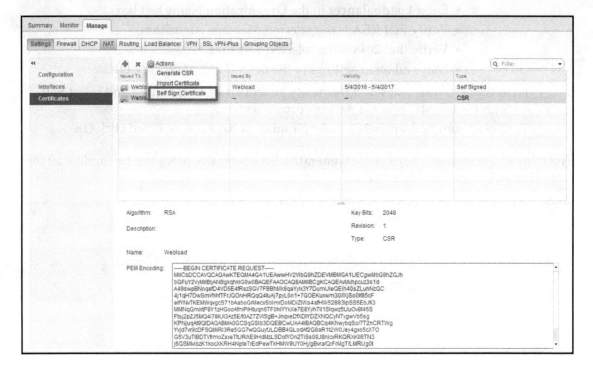

Setting up a load balancer

We will perform the following steps in the same order to set up and test a load balancer.

- Set global option for the load balancer
- Create an application profile
- Create a service monitor to define health check performance
- Create a server pool
- Test the load balancer

Setting global options

The procedure for setting global options for the load balancer is as follows:

1. Log in to the vSphere web client.
2. Click **Networking & Security** and then click **NSX Edges**.
3. Double-click an NSX Edge.
4. Click **Manage** and then click the **Load Balancer** tab.
5. Click **Edit**.
6. Select the check boxes next to the options you want to enable:
   - **Enable Load balancer**: Allows the NSX Edge load balancer to distribute traffic to internal servers for load balancing
   - **Enable Service Insertion**: Allows the load balancer to work with third-party vendor appliances.
   - **Acceleration Enabled**: When enabled, the NSX Edge load balancer uses the faster L4 LB engine rather than the L7 LB engine.
   - **Logging**: The NSX Edge load balancer collects traffic logs. You can also choose the log level.
7. Click **OK**.

Creating an application profile

Since we have enabled the load balancer service, in this step, we will configure for HTTPS traffic:

1. Under the **Manage** tab, click **Load Balancer**.
2. In the load balancer category panel, select **Global Configuration**.
3. Click **Edit**, on the right-hand side of the global configuration page.
4. On the **Edit load balancer global configuration** page, select the **Enable Load Balancer** checkbox and click **OK**. Select the certificate that we created earlier and leave all other fields at the default value.
5. The **Insert X-Forwarded-For HTTP header** helps you identify the IP address of a client when you use an HTTP load balancer.
6. In the load balancer category panel, select **Application Profiles**.

7. Above the top panel, click the green plus sign to open the **New Profile** dialog box, and perform the following actions:
    1. Enter **Web-Server** in the **Name** text box.
    2. Click **HTTPS**.
    3. Leave all other fields at the default value and click **OK**.

The following screenshot shows the **Application Profile Configuration** for the load balancer:

Creating a service monitor

We can create a service monitor to define health check parameters for a particular type of network traffic. When you associate a service monitor with a pool, the pool members are monitored according to the service monitor parameters. The following screenshot shows the default service monitoring pools:

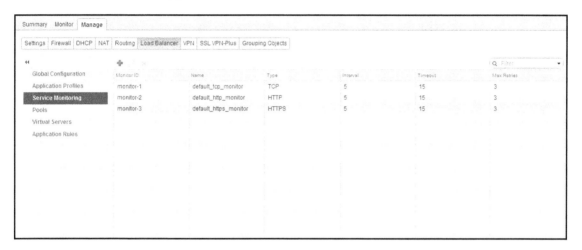

Creating a server pool

In this step, we will create a round-robin server pool that contains the two web server virtual machines as members:

1. Above the top panel, click the green plus sign to open the **New Pool** dialog box, and perform the following actions:
2. In the load balancer category panel, select **Pools**.
    1. Enter **Web-Pool** in the **Name** text box.
    2. Verify that the **Algorithm** selection is **ROUND-ROBIN**.
    3. In the monitoring selection, we can either select **NONE**, one of the default monitoring pools, or something that we manually created.
    4. Below **Members**, click the green plus sign to open the **New Member** dialog box, and add the first server.
    5. Click **OK** to close the **New Member** dialog box.
    6. Under **Members**, click the green plus sign to open the **New Member** dialog box, and add a second server.
    7. Click **OK** to close the **New Member** dialog box.

8. Click **OK** to close the **New Pool** dialog box.
3. In the Name field enter **Web -01a**.
4. In the IP Address field enter **172.16.10.11**.
5. In **Port** field enter **443** in the text box.
6. Leave all other settings at the default value.
7. Repeat the same steps and add our second web server, `172.16.20.11`. The following screenshot shows the pool settings that we configured:

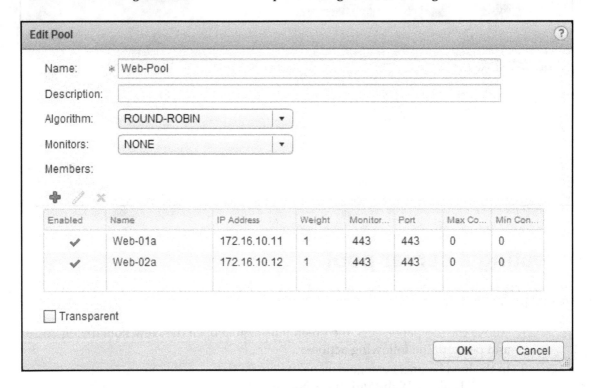

Creating a virtual server

The virtual server is positioned on the external network attached to the uplink interface of the perimeter:

1. In the load balancer category panel, select **Virtual Servers**.
2. Above the top panel, click the green plus sign to open the **New Virtual Server** dialog box, and perform the following actions:
    1. Verify that the **Enabled** check box is selected.

2. Enter **VIP** in the **Name** text box.
3. Enter **192.168.100.9** in the **IP Address** text box.
4. Select **HTTPS** from the **Protocol** drop-down menu.
5. Verify that the **Port** setting has changed to 443.
6. Select **Web-Pool** from the **Default Pool** drop-down menu.
7. Verify that the **Application Profile** selection is **Web-Server**.
8. Leave all other settings at the default value and click **OK**

The following screenshot depicts the virtual server configuration for the web-pool that we are trying to load balance:

We are not leveraging an **application** rule in the load balancing setup. With application rules, we have the flexibility to specify HTTP/HTTPS redirection; regardless of the URL, the traffic will always redirect based on the rules. All we need to do now for testing is just go ahead and enter the VIP 192.168.100.9 in the browser, and we should see the traffic getting redirected to one of the web servers.

The following screenshot shows the load balancing done against web-sv-02a:

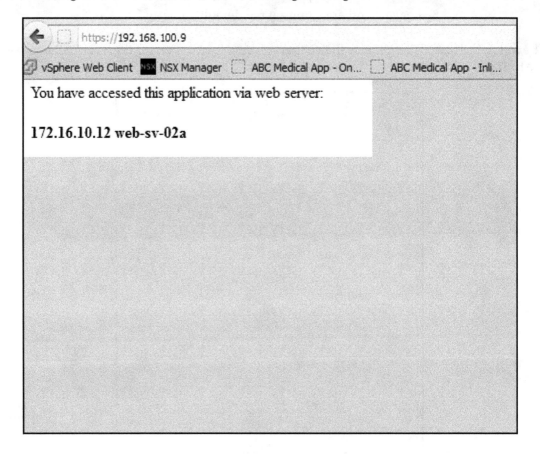

I personally hate learning things from looking at a GUI. CLI is my best friend, and I have captured a debug output of our load balancing scenario with the lab topology to ensure that the concepts are crystal clear for everyone:

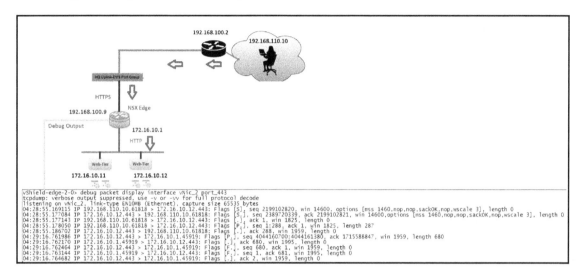

That concludes the topic of load balancing, and we all know that we certainly need a working NSX Edge instance to load balance any traffic.

Virtual Private Network

NSX Edge supports several types of VPN service, such as SSL-VPN, L2-VPN, and IPsec VPN. They are as follows:

- **SSL VPN-plus**: The prime reason someone would go for an SSL VPN connection would be for users (roaming profiles) who need to access private networks that are behind a perimeter device.

- **IPsec VPN**: NSX supports site to site VPN between the NSX Edge gateway and most of the third-party IPsec VPN devices.

- **L2 VPN**: In the current cloud era, we have a lot of use cases where an on-premises network needs an extension all the way to another site, which can be a private cloud or any other public cloud service, such as vCloud Air, AWS, and Azure. Please don't confuse this with a direct connect solution. Virtual machines in L2 VPN will be on the same subnet, irrespective of being moved between the sites.

Let's discuss these topics a bit more in depth to learn about their features and where NSX would fit, and finally, we will focus on a few design decisions.

SSL VPN

The NSX SSL VPN feature provides remote users a secure connection to a private network, which is residing behind an NSX Edge gateway. We can either have a web-based connection, or we need to install an SSL client and access the private network. Behind the scenes, traffic will be tunneled and securely directed to private networks. The following steps would be done in the same order to configure an SSL VPN connection:

1. Configure SSL VPN server settings.
2. Add an IP pool.
3. Add a private network.
4. Add authentication.
5. Add an installation package.
6. Add a user.
7. Verify all the configurations and enable SSL VPN.

The following figure depicts three sites (A, B, C), which are in need of connecting to other sites through SSL-VPN, IPSEC, and L2 VPN setups:

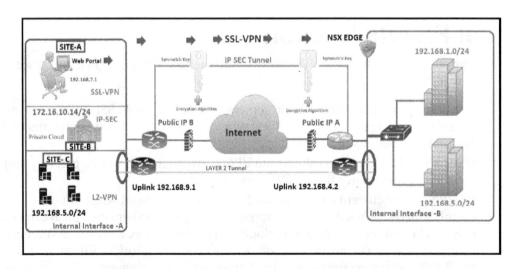

We will start with SITE-A's SSL VPN configuration.

Configure SSL VPN server settings

As mentioned previously, we need to follow Steps 1 to 7 to configure SSL-VPN settings:

1. In the **SSL VPN-Plus** tab, select **Server Settings** from the left-hand panel.
2. Click **Change**.
3. Select the **IPv4 Address** or **IPv6 Address**.
4. Edit the port number if required. This port number is required to configure the installation package.
5. Select the encryption method.
6. From the **Server certificate** table, select the server certificate that you want to add. This is an optional step; adding to that, let's not get embarrassed that we are seeing a web-load SSL certificate. This is the same certificate that we created earlier during the SSL-load balancer topic.
7. Click **OK**.

The following screenshot shows the SSL VPN server settings:

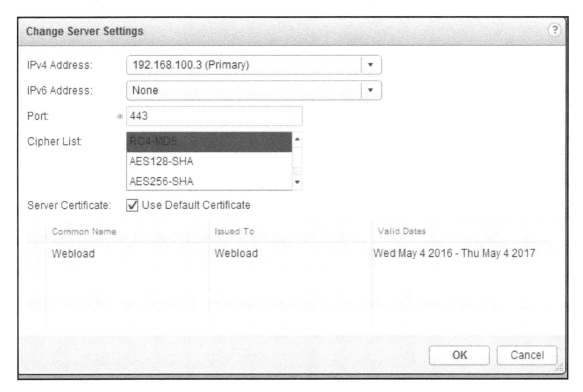

Adding ID pool

The whole purpose of adding this pool is to assign a **Virtual IP** (**VIP**) from the pool of IP addresses to the remote user. The following screenshot depicts an IP pool page:

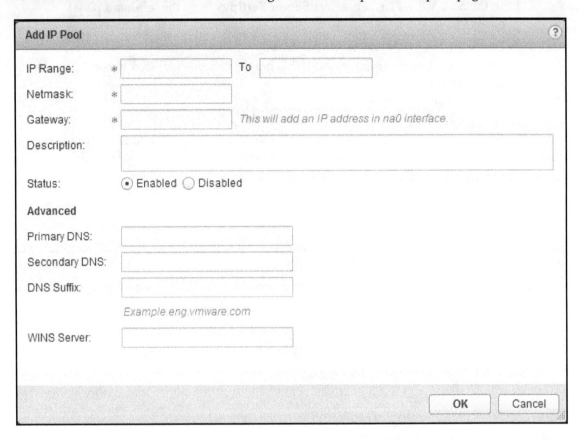

In our example, we are taking the range as 192.168.170.2 to 192.168.170.254 and the gateway as 192.168.170.1. DNS/WINS settings are optional; hence, we are skipping that configuration.

Private network

The private network is the network that we want our remote users to connect to and access. The following screenshot depicts the private network configuration. We are taking 192.168.1.0/24 as our network for SSL VPN access:

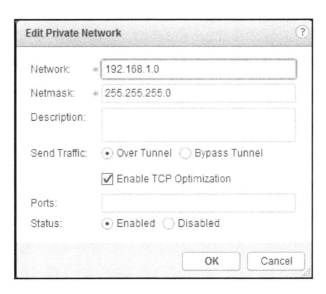

Please take a look at the following steps:

1. **Add authentication**: External authentication servers like AD, LDAP, Radius, or RSA are supported, or we can simply create a local user and use the same local user name and password to connect to the private network.

2. **Add an installation package**: We can create an installation package of the SSL-VPN client for remote users based on the type of operating system from which we need to access the private network. There are several logon settings we can select during the package selection.

3. **Add a user**: Since we have already added the authentication method, we can go ahead and add those users for accessing the private network.

4. **Enable SSL VPN service**: After verifying the entire configuration, we need to enable the SSL VPN service by switching to the **SSL VPN-Plus** tab. Select **Dashboard** from the left-hand panel. The following screenshot shows a **Service enabled successfully** message:

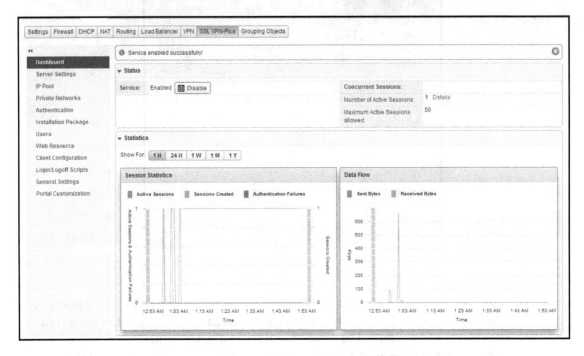

Now that we have successfully enabled an SSL-service, remote user (192.168.7.1) can initiate an SSL-VPN connection to the private network (192.168.1.0/24) after authentication, based on the type of authentication we selected earlier. There are several ways in which we can check the SSL session. The best and easiest way would be from the client machine itself (192.168.7.1), by doing a **route lookup** on the local operating system; we would see a new route added all the way to the private network. With that, we are moving on to IPsec VPN for **Site-B**.

IPsec VPN

NSX Edge Gateway supports Site-Site VPN between NSX Edge and remote sites. In a nutshell, the original packet will be authenticated and encrypted, and it will be encapsulated with an **Encapsulation Security Payload (ESP)** header, trailer, and authentication data. The following screenshot depicts initial IPsec VPN configuration:

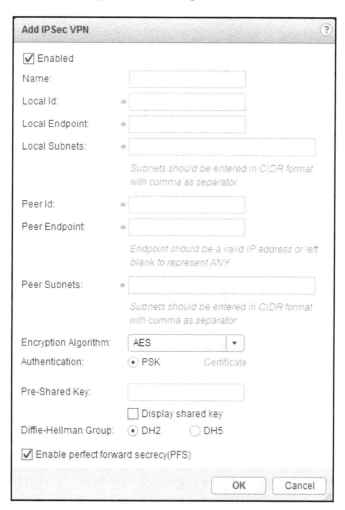

Since we already have a topology shared earlier, the requirement is to establish an IPsec tunnel between Site-B and the remote site (192.168.5.0/24). Let's get started.

Following is the procedure for configuring IPsec:

1. Log in to the vSphere web client.
2. Click **Networking & Security** and then click **NSX Edges**.
3. Double-click an NSX Edge.
4. Click the **Monitor** tab and then click the **VPN** tab.
5. Click **IPSec VPN**.
6. Click the add icon.
7. Type a name for the IPsec VPN.
8. Type the IP address of the NSX Edge instance in **Local Id**. This will be the **Peer Id** on the remote site.
9. Type the IP address of the local endpoint.

If you are adding an IP-to-IP tunnel using a pre-shared key, the local ID and local endpoint IP can be the same.

10. Type the subnets to share between the sites in CIDR format. Use a comma separator to type multiple subnets.
11. Type the **Peer Id** to uniquely identify the peer site. For peers using certificate authentication, this ID must be the common name in the peer's certificate. For PSK peers, this ID can be any string. VMware recommends that you use the public IP address of the VPN or a FQDN for the VPN service as the peer ID.
12. Type the IP address of the peer site in **Peer Endpoint**. If you leave this blank, NSX Edge waits for the peer device to request a connection.
13. Type the internal IP address of the peer subnet in CIDR format. Use a comma separator to type multiple subnets.
14. Select the **Encryption Algorithm**.

Pre-Shared Key (PSK): This indicates that the secret key shared between NSX Edge and the peer site is to be used for authentication. The secret key can be a string with a maximum length of 128 bytes. NSX IPsec VPN supports symmetric keys. **Certificate**: This indicates that the certificate defined at the global level is to be used for authentication.

15. Type in the shared key if anonymous sites are to connect to the VPN service.
16. Click **Display Shared Key** to display the key on the peer site.

17. In **Diffie-Hellman (DH) Group**, select the cryptography scheme that will allow the peer site and the NSX Edge to establish a shared secret over an insecure communications channel.

18. Edit the default MTU if required.

19. Select whether to enable or disable the **Perfect Forward Secrecy** (**PFS**) threshold. In IPsec negotiations, PFS ensures that each new cryptographic key is unrelated to any previous key.

20. Click **OK**.

21. Enable VPN.

22. As per our topology, we have updated our IPsec configuration in the Edge. Once we configure the partner device, the IPsec tunnel will get established:

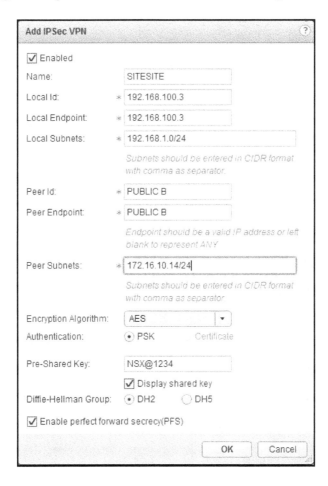

The IKE phase 1 parameters used by the NSX Edge include:

- Main mode
- AES / AES 256 preferred / TripleDES /
- SHA-1
- MODP (DH) group 2 (MODP1024 bits)
- Pre-shared secret [Configurable]
- SA lifetime of 28800 seconds (eight hours) with no kilobytes rekeying
- ISAKMP aggressive mode disabled

The IKE phase 2 parameters supported by NSX Edge include:

- AES / AES 256 Preferred / TripleDES / [Will match the Phase 1 setting]
- SHA-1
- ESP tunnel mode
- MODP (DH) group 2 (MODP1024 bits)
- Perfect forwarding secrecy for rekeying
- SA lifetime of 3600 seconds (one hour) with no kilobytes rekeying
- Selectors for all IP protocols and all ports between the two networks using IPv4 subnets

L2 VPN

L2 VPN allows us to configure a tunnel between two sites. As I said earlier, virtual machines will be on the same subnet irrespective of where they are moving. As per our topology, we need to establish a L2-VPN between Site-C and remote site 192.168.5.0/24. In our example, we are taking Site-C as the L2 VPN server, and the remote site is the L2 VPN client. The L2 VPN server is the source NSX Edge server to which destination L2 VPN Client is getting connected.

Prerequisites

The internal IP address assigned to the L2 VPN server and client must be different. They can be on the same subnet.

Following is the procedure for L2 VPN server:

1. Log in to the vSphere web client.

2. Click **Networking & Security** and then click **NSX Edges**.
3. Double-click an NSX Edge.
4. Click the **Manage** tab and then click the **VPN** tab.
5. Click **L2 VPN**, select **Server**, and click **Change**.
6. Expand **Server Details**.
7. In **Listener IP**, type the primary or secondary IP address of an external interface of the NSX Edge. In our example, the IP would be 192.168.9.1.
8. The default port for the L2 VPN service is **443**. Edit this if required.
9. Select the encryption method.
10. Select the internal interface of the NSX Edge that is being stretched .This interface must be connected to a DV port group or logical switch.
11. Type a description.
12. Expand **User Details** and type the username and password.
13. In server certificates, do one of the following:
    1. Select **Use System Generated Certificate** to use a self signed certificate for authentication.
    2. Select the signed certificate to be used for authentication.
14. Click **OK**:

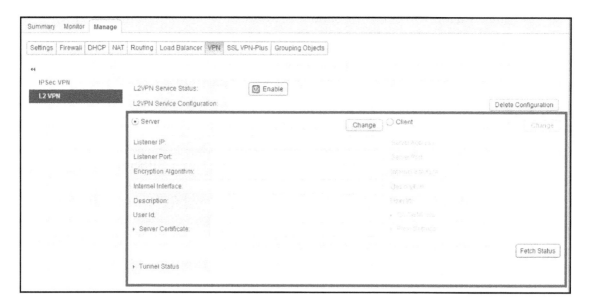

Listener IP: 192.168.9.1
Listener Port: 443
Encryption Algorithm: AES256-SHA
Internal Interface: Internal Interface-A
User Id: vpn-user
Server Certificate: TEST.LOCAL

To configure the L2-VPN client, all we need to update is the server address to which the client is supposed to be connected, and the internal interface that needs to be stretched. Apart from these details, the rest of the configuration is the same, and the L2 tunnel will be up and running after that

- **L2VPN Service Status: Enabled**
- **Server Address: 192.168.9.1**
- **Server Port: 443**
- **Internal Interface: Internal Interface-B**
- **User Id: vpn-user**

Design decisions while configuring VPN

The following are a few key points we should be aware of while configuring the VPN:

- Route-based VPN is not supported, NSX Edge supports only policy-based VPN
- We can have a maximum of 64 tunnels across a maximum of 10 sites
- NAT-traversal is supported in VPN configuration
- Overlapping of subnets is not allowed
- Route summarization is supported for both peer and local subnets
- Dynamic routing through IPsec tunnels is not supported
- NSX Edge supports pre-shared key and certificate-based authentication.
- There are a few exceptions with special characters in a pre-shared key that I have seen with a few third-party vendors. Hence, watch out for special characters.

That concludes VPN key design decisions, and it is always advisable not to deviate and start configuring VPN from what the product doesn't support.

DHCP relay

Dynamic Host Configuration Protocol automatically assigns an IP address. This is something we all know. But there is certainly a drawback with that model: the DHCP server and client should be on the same broadcast domain. In a nutshell, the DHCP relay agent relays DHCP messages between client and server on different networks. This is a new feature, which was added in **NSX 6.1** and can be applied on **DLR or NSX Edge**. In earlier versions of NSX and VCNS, we were limited to configuring traditional DHCP servers. It is important to know that we cannot have overlapping subnets. But what if we need the same IP every time a virtual machine boots? NSX DHCP static binding would do the trick in that case. We can simply bind the IP with the MAC of a virtual machine.

Summary

We started this chapter with an introduction to NSX Edge, and later, we covered routing protocols and NSX Edge services, use cases, and a few design considerations. This was certainly a lengthy topic, and the whole purpose of explaining the topics with a few labs and topologies was to make it as informative as possible. I strongly believe that in the near future, we will see lot of new features getting added to NSX Edge services. For example, NSX Edge being a Perimeter Device, we would be more than happy to see WAN acceleration features or Policy Based Routing.

With the skills that we have gained so far, we are good to start with our next chapter, on NSX security features and design decisions. We will have a close look at NSX security policies, groups, and a few use cases.

6
NSX Security Features

Traditionally, isolating and securing a network was done at the perimeter level of any data center, which was an error-prone and time-consuming activity. In the current Software Defined Data Center world, where most workloads are dynamic, we need better control over the security feature, and at the same time we expect configuration and management of these tasks to be automated without compromising any security features. If there is a virtual machine migration from one server to another server all my polices should move along with that irrespective of Layer 2 and Layer 3 boundaries. But the real question would be, is that really possible? In this chapter, we will discuss how NSX has changed the view of modern-day data center security. We will be covering the following topics with some classic examples:

- NSX Distributed Firewall
- NSX Service Composer
- NSX Distributed Firewall monitoring
- NSX SpoofGuard
- DFW takeaways

NSX Distributed Firewall

NSX **Distributed Firewall** (**DFW**) focuses on East-West traffic and NSX Edge firewall focuses on North-South traffic. Those of us who remember the vCloud network security days will feel like this is an enhancement of the vShield app. Okay! For now, I would certainly agree with that; it is certainly an enhanced feature-rich version of the vShield app firewall. But the app demands that you run a dedicated firewall VM for each host and the virtual machine remains protected irrespective of where they are moving. Apart from the fact that it demands a hypervisor-specific firewall (FW) virtual machine, it was a featureless firewall and installation and troubleshooting was also slightly tedious. NSX Distributed Firewall is a hypervisor kernel-embedded firewall and policies are totally virtualization-aware. What does that mean? We can apply policies on vCenter objects such as data centers and clusters and virtual machine names and tags, and network constructs such as IP/VLAN/VXLAN addresses. What if we have the same firewall rule added in NSX Edge and Distributed Firewall? Which policy would be enforced first? There are two answers to that question. If the traffic is going out from the virtual machine, certainly the distributed firewall rule will be checked first, primarily because it is a VNIC-level firewall policy. However, if traffic is coming into the virtual data center, NSX Edge, our perimeter device, will be the first point of firewall rule table checking and later there would be a VNIC-level filtering also. Time to ask a few questions and justify why it is a feature-rich firewall:

- Can we have a dynamic FW rule creation based on the virtual name or operating system name?
- I have a domain user **A** and we need to **allow** and **block** a few rules based on user access **A**. Is that achievable?
- I have two tenants and we are using IPV4 and IPV6 respectively; can we leverage the Distributed Firewall feature irrespective of the IP stack?
- Can we monitor the network activity between two virtual machines based on the firewall rule? This will ensure our rules are working as expected or we can take proactive action if required.
- I'm migrating my virtual machine from cluster A to cluster B; will it retain the security/firewall policies? Do I need to add/delete any security/firewall settings in the physical network?
- Can we implement a few network security policies without changing/impacting our existing physical network topology?

The preceding questions are not a complete list. However, these are few key concerns for now, apart from being keen to know if we have a security feature X when we leverage an NSX distributed firewall, the fundamental problem is the question of whether I can switch my traditional physical-network-based security controls to the NSX world so that my features and policies are more virtualization-aware or, one more ask is, are they application aware policies with visibility over users, process, usage, and so on? Don't get me wrong, we are not taking/removing all the physical network security settings and replicating them in the NSX world. All we need is a better secured network virtualized platform. NSX Distributed Firewall provides a micro-segmentation feature which resolves a lot of network security challenges. Since the firewall modules are running inside the ESXi host, we will always get a better throughput and policy configuration, deletion and monitoring all can be done from one single management console—vSphere web client. Before discussing firewall rules and how they work, let's understand what components are involved and how they communicate with each other. As we can see from the following diagram, we have vSphere web client, NSX Manager, and vSphere farm with all the VIBS loaded. By connecting to vCenter Server through web client, we can create security policies and NSX Manager will push the policies to vSphere Servers. **VMware Service Insertion Platform** (VSIP), which is a module within DFW, will apply the policy to underlying virtual machines. Any new generation or traditional port-based firewall will have an intelligent rule table and NSX DFW is of no exception. There are two tables associated with DFW:

- Rule table
- Connection table

While the rule table maintains all the rules, the connection table will keep track of active connections based on the type of rules that we have created:

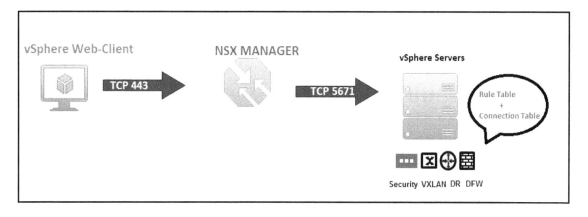

Now that we have a fundamental understanding of what Distributed Firewall is, it is equally important to know that DFW is fully virtualization-aware firewall and we can set firewall rules at the following vCenter Server objects:

- Data center
- Cluster
- vSwitch Port Group
- Distributed Switch Port Group
- Virtual app(vAPP)
- Resource pool
- Virtual machine
- vNIC
- Logical switch
- Security Group
- IP Sets
- NSX Service Composer

NSX Service Composer is a built-in feature which allows you to configure security services, firewall rules, and security policies with the help of security groups and security policies. We can create security groups and security policies and can apply a combination of security groups and security policies using NSX Service Composer, which is certainly a great way of automating rule/policy creation tasks. In a nutshell, we are doing two tasks and the final result is the automation of network security in the NSX world:

Deploy + Apply = Network Security Automation

But the question is, What are we going to deploy and where are we going to apply that? For that, we need to understand what security groups and security policies are.

Security groups

A security group is where we define what type of assets we want to protect and we can define the group with the **dynamic way** of selecting an asset or we could simply create a **static membership** group. We will go back and read our questionnaire section in this chapter:

Can we have dynamic rule creation based on the virtual name or operating system name?

That gives us clarity on why dynamic membership would be a key factor while creating security groups. In a nutshell, when we create a Dynamic Membership Group with selection criteria *Include All Operating System of windows flavor and apply the Security Group with a Security Policy that will one the easiest way in which we would have created and Secured our Virtual Machines with the intelligence of DFW firewall.*

Security policies

Security policies are combinations of security services and firewall rules. Policies can be a combination of antivirus, data security, vulnerability, network introspection, and firewall rules.

Okay! But what if we need to create a dynamic group, while excluding virtual machines running on one specific logic switch and given that all these configurations should be part of a single security group? This is the real power of security groups: all these configurations can be part of a single security group and in that case our security group will be like this:

Dynamic Inclusion + Static Inclusion (if required, we can still have a static inclusion list) – Static Exclusion = Security Group.

Creating a service group

With a basic understanding of security groups and security policies, we will go ahead and discuss one of the security requirements to show the power of this feature. Let's have a look at one of the network requirements for securing the traffic with DFW features and we will discuss the lab exercise. As per the following topology, we have our three-tier application running on three logical switches and a transit network:

- App-Tier-01
- Web-Tier-01
- DB-Tier-01
- Transit network

In the following diagram, by leveraging NSX DFW we will disable the ICMP traffic in the Web-Tier logic switch and the final result will be that web servers running in logical switch Web-Tier-01 will block ICMP traffic:

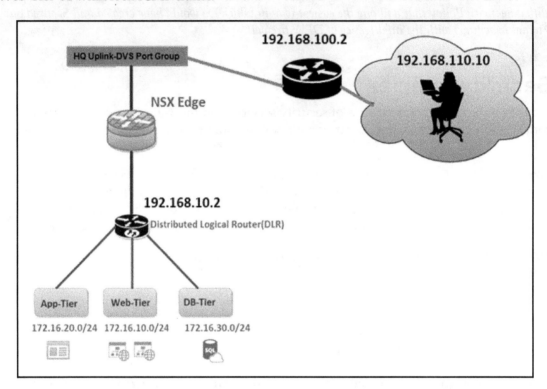

Before we start, let's do a simple ping test to confirm whether ICMP is allowed. The following screenshot depicts successful ICMP traffic between web-01a and web-02a connected to same logical switch Web Tier-01:

```
[root@web-02a ~]# ping -c 2 172.16.10.11
PING 172.16.10.11 (172.16.10.11) 56(84) bytes of data.
64 bytes from 172.16.10.11: icmp_seq=1 ttl=64 time=5.53 ms
64 bytes from 172.16.10.11: icmp_seq=2 ttl=64 time=1.11 ms

--- 172.16.10.11 ping statistics ---
2 packets transmitted, 2 received, 0% packet loss, time 1002ms
rtt min/avg/max/mdev = 1.112/3.323/5.534/2.211 ms
[root@web-02a ~]#
```

For configuring a Distributed Firewall rule, we have two methods:

- By selecting **Firewall** | **Networking & Security** | **Firewall**
- By selecting **Service Composer** | **Networking & Security** | **Service Composer**

In this example, I'm leveraging Service Composer. Let's create a security group with the name **Web Security-Group**:

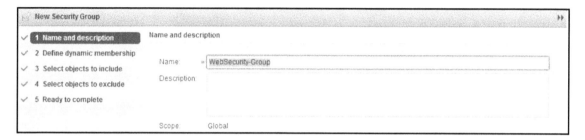

In the dynamic membership list, we are not selecting any options. However, it is worth focusing on the **Criteria Details** option to get a clear picture of what options are available for defining a dynamic membership group as shown in the following screenshot. For example, if we select VM name in the following criteria list and mention Windows in white text box and create a Security Group. Any existing/future virtual machines which are getting deployed in vCenter Server will be applied with the DFW policy. Highly powerful feature as it ease lot of repeated task when same set of polices are required for a group of virtual machines also down the line adding and deletion of polices to same group is a one click task:

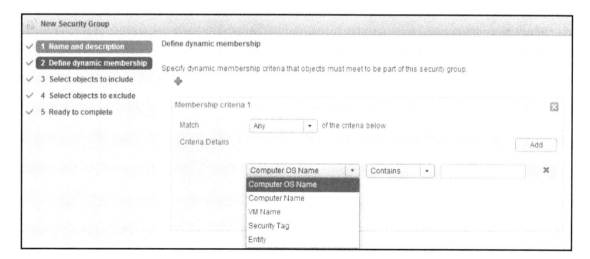

In the static inclusion list, we set **Object Type** to **Logical Switch** so that we can apply the policy on the **Web-Tier-01** logical switch as shown in the following screenshot:

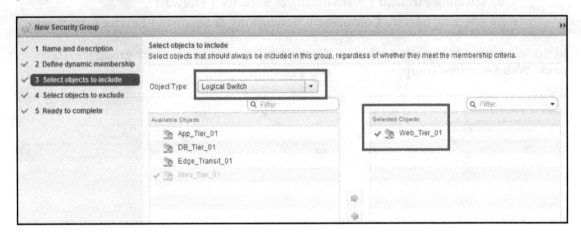

What next? I have intentionally connected a **Linux VM** to our **Web-Tier** and the idea is to exclude only Linux from the security group policy that we are creating. Even though we are creating a security group at Logical Switch level, we can still filter our policy in such a way by mentioning a exclusion criteria. In a nutshell, polices are applied at logical switch level, however it is not applied to all the virtual machines connected to same logical switch. As we can see from following screenshot, we have set **Object Type** to **Virtual Machine** and excluded **Linux-01a**:

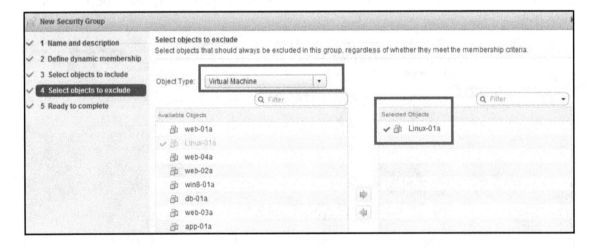

With that step, we are done with security group creation and we will see the web security group created under **Service Composer** | **Networking & Security** | **Service Composer**. I have explicitly highlighted the virtual machine as I want everyone's attention on the virtual machine number, which is showing as **1**. Using the same step, we will create another security group called **Web2Security** and in the static inclusion we will include the **Web-02a** virtual machine.

So let's revise the two security group rules with our example:

- Security Group (Web Security-Group) = Dynamic Inclusion (Not Selected Anything) + Static Inclusion (Selected Web-Tier Logical Switch) – Static Exclusion (Excluded Linux VM)
- Security Group (Web2Security) = Dynamic Inclusion (Not Selected Anything) + Static Inclusion (Web-02a) – Static Exclusion (Not Selected anything)

The following screenshot depicts two security groups that we created and we can see the VM count also showing there:

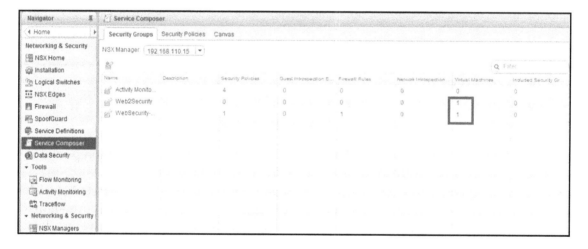

Creating a security policy

As we have discussed earlier, policies are groups of security services, such as antivirus, IPS/IDS solution, and DFW rules.

Before creating policies, we need to prioritize the policy with a weight attribute if required. The whole purpose of this feature is that, at times, objects (in our example, let's take a virtual machine as an object) will be part of multiple policies. Based on which policy has a higher weight attribute, that policy will take precedence over lower-weight attributes. In addition to that, if the policy that we are creating receives services from another security policy, we need to select the parent policy.

The following screenshot depicts a security policy being created; we name it **Web Security-Group**:

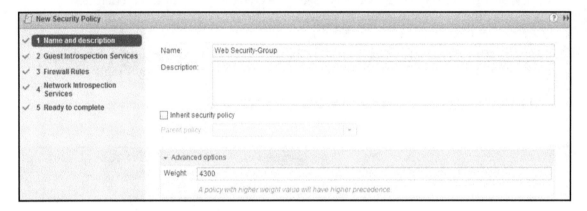

Since we are not leveraging guest introspection and network introspection services in this example, I'm skipping that configuration and moving directly to the firewall rule. Both configurations will be extremely useful for the following scenarios:

- Endpoint services are required for data security or third-party solution provider services such as antivirus or vulnerability management services.
- To detect sensitive data such as **Payment Card Industry** (PCI), **Protected Health Information** (PHI), and **Personally Identifiable Information** (PII) information in our environment, we can create data security policies. When we run a scan, data security identifies data that violates the regulations in your policy will be **blocked** with brilliance of firewall policies.
- Network introspection services that monitor your network, such as IPS.

Let's have a closer look at the firewall source and destination rules:

- **Source**: Policy Security Group
- **Destination**: Web2Security Group
- **Service**: We are blocking all ICMP traffic (total 4 ICMP traffic selected which we will see very shortly)

The following screenshot depicts the preceding rules:

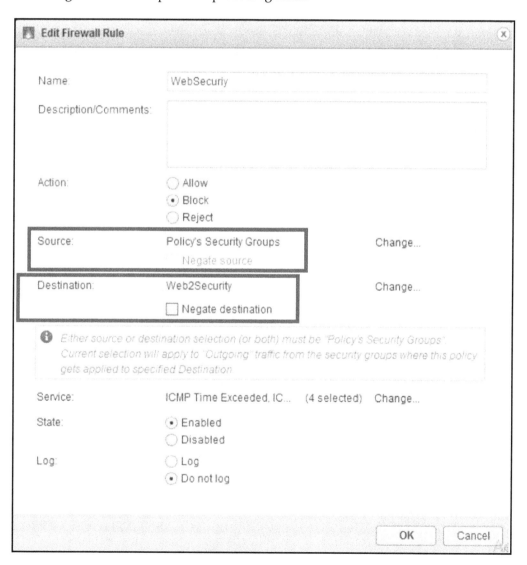

Now that our security policies and security groups have been created, we can simply apply our policy to the **security group** which we created earlier by clicking on the **Apply Policy** option, which is portrayed in the following screenshot:

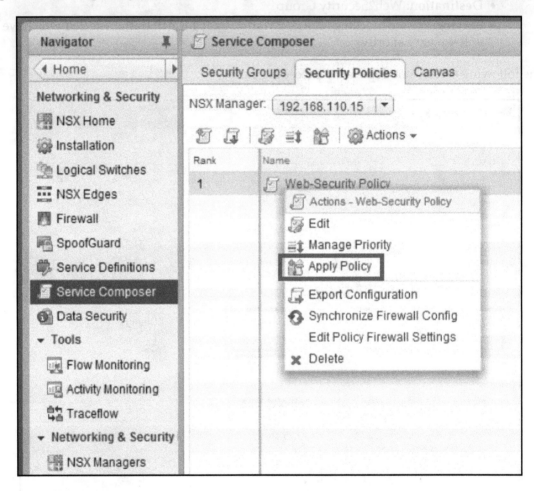

While applying the security policy, NSX will show us all **Security Groups** that have been created and we need to ensure we are applying it against the correct security group. Selecting the wrong security group will have a major impact on network traffic. Also, we can see a **Synchronize Firewall Config** option just below **Apply Policy**. Any time we modify a policy, it is recommended to synchronize the firewall configuration. A good sign with the latest release of NSX 6.2.3 is there is an out-of-sync security policy alarm which will be generated if a security policy is out of sync. But watch out for previous versions of NSX Manager as we will never know if the policy is out of sync unless a problem is reported and we isolate the same after troubleshooting.

Testing firewall rules

What next? Well, if we have been alert so far, we will see these rules getting populated in **Firewall | Networking & Security | Firewall**. The following screenshot depicts the WebSecurity rule that we created for:

- **Source: WebSecurity-Group (Web-01a)**
- **Destination: Web2Security (Web-02a)**
- **Services**: 4 ICMP protocols and **Action** is **Block**

Time to test what we have configured so far and I will show you the detailed firewall summary on the ESXi host. As we can see from the following screenshot, we have an SSH session to the web-02a machine and we are able to ping 172.16.10.11 (web-01a):

```
[root@web-02a ~]# ping -c 2 172.16.10.11
PING 172.16.10.11 (172.16.10.11) 56(84) bytes of data.
64 bytes from 172.16.10.11: icmp_seq=1 ttl=64 time=1.28 ms
64 bytes from 172.16.10.11: icmp_seq=2 ttl=64 time=0.582 ms

--- 172.16.10.11 ping statistics ---
2 packets transmitted, 2 received, 0% packet loss, time 1002ms
rtt min/avg/max/mdev = 0.582/0.931/1.280/0.349 ms
[root@web-02a ~]#
```

Now, if we do a ping test from `web-01a` to `web-02a,` as shown in the following screenshot, the result would be a failure, primarily because of the **ICMP DROP** rules that we have created:

```
[root@web-01a ~]# ping -c 5 172.16.10.12
PING 172.16.10.12 (172.16.10.12) 56(84) bytes of data.

--- 172.16.10.12 ping statistics ---
5 packets transmitted, 0 received, 100% packet loss, time 14000ms

[root@web-01a ~]#
```

I strongly believe our DFW basics are crystal-clear. Even though we have a troubleshooting chapter coming up, I'm very excited to show you an informative output that we can check and view from the underlying host. All we need to do is to take an SSH session to the ESXi host wherein our web servers are running and issue the following command:

> `summarize-dvfilter`

Distributed Virtual Filter is the module that monitors the outgoing and incoming traffic that is protected by NSX DFW. So this command would display the same output. The following command output is for the Web-02a virtual machine and let's make a note of the name of the vNic slot 2 associated with the `VM - nic-60841-eth0-vmware-sfw.2:`

```
world 68041 vmm0:web-02a vcUuid:'50 2e 6d 0e 07 a4 a4 d6-0e 16 4d 12 a5 cf 1e 52'
 port 33554445 web-02a.eth0
  vNic slot 2
   name: nic-68041-eth0-vmware-sfw.2
   agentName: vmware-sfw
   state: IOChain Attached
   vmState: Detached
   failurePolicy: failClosed
   slowPathID: none
   filter source: Dynamic Filter Creation
  vNic slot 1
   name: nic-68041-eth0-dvfilter-generic-vmware-swsec.1
   agentName: dvfilter-generic-vmware-swsec
   state: IOChain Attached
   vmState: Detached
   failurePolicy: failClosed
   slowPathID: none
   filter source: Alternate Opaque Channel
```

As we can see that the preceding command and output don't give any information on all the DFW rules associated with that virtual machine, let's display the rules associated with the name `nic-60841-eth0-vmware-sfw.2`. Issue the following command in the same host:

```
Vsipioctl getfwrules -f nic-60841-eth0-vmware-sfw.2
```

The following screenshot clearly depicts all the rules. I have marked the **DROP** rule and we have a total of four rules, which are just the ICMP rules we created a few minutes ago:

```
[root@esx-01a:~] vsipioctl getfwrules -f nic-37282-eth0-vmware-sfw.2
ruleset domain-c33 {
  # Filter rules
  rule 1005 at 1 inout protocol any from any to addrset ip-vm-321 reject;
  rule 1007 at 2 inout protocol icmp icmptype 3 from addrset ip-securitygroup-10 to addrset ip-securitygroup-12 drop;
  rule 1007 at 3 inout protocol icmp icmptype 0 from addrset ip-securitygroup-10 to addrset ip-securitygroup-12 drop;
  rule 1007 at 4 inout protocol icmp icmptype 11 from addrset ip-securitygroup-10 to addrset ip-securitygroup-12 drop;
  rule 1007 at 5 inout protocol icmp icmptype 8 from addrset ip-securitygroup-10 to addrset ip-securitygroup-12 drop;
  rule 1003 at 6 inout protocol ipv6-icmp icmptype 136 from any to any accept;
  rule 1003 at 7 inout protocol ipv6-icmp icmptype 135 from any to any accept;
  rule 1002 at 8 inout protocol udp from any to any port 68 accept;
  rule 1002 at 9 inout protocol udp from any to any port 67 accept;
  rule 1001 at 10 inout protocol any from any to any accept;
}

ruleset domain-c33_L2 {
  # Filter rules
  rule 1004 at 1 inout ethertype any from any to any accept;
}
```

As I said earlier, the complete centralized management of Distributed Firewall is done from vSphere web client and, as far as rules are concerned, we will provide a name, source and destination entities, type of service, action required, and where the rules are enforced. In addition to normal rule creation, DFW also supports an identity-based firewall.

Understanding identity-based firewall rules

Let me reiterate our second query that we had when we discussed DFW:

I have a domain user A and we need to allow and block a few rules based on user access A. Is that achievable?

With an identity-based firewall, we can define firewall rules based on **Active Directory (AD)** groups. Obviously, there are few prerequisites and limitations when we use an identity-based firewall, which we will discuss in a short while. First and foremost, we need to register AD with NSX Manager.

Procedure for AD registration

We will follow these steps to register the AD on NSX Manager:

1. Firstly, we will log in to vSphere web client.
2. Click **Networking & Security** and then click **NSX Managers**.
3. Click an NSX Manager in the **Name** column and then click the **Manage** tab.
4. Click the **Domain** tab and then click on the add domain icon.
5. In the **Add Domain** dialog box, enter the fully qualified domain name and netBIOS name for the domain. The following figure depicts the preceding steps:

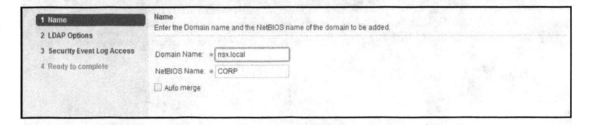

6. In the **LDAP Options** page, specify the domain controller that the domain is to be synchronized with and select the protocol.
7. Edit the port number if required.
8. Enter the user credentials for the domain account. This user must be able to access the directory tree structure.

   The following figure shows the LDAP configuration that needs to be filled in during the configuration time:

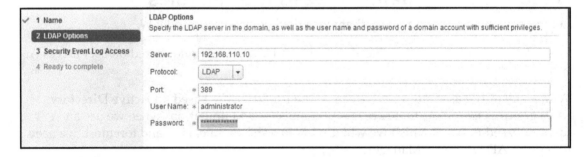

9. In the **Security Event Log Access** page, select the connection method to access security event logs on the specified LDAP server. Change the port number if required.

10. Select **Use Domain Credentials** to use the LDAP server user credentials. To specify an alternate domain account for log access, un-select **Use Domain Credentials** and specify the user name and password. The specified account must be able to read the security event logs on the domain controller.
11. Click **Next**.
12. In the **Ready to complete** page, review the settings you entered.
13. Click **Finish**.

Once after configuring required AD details as shown in the above steps, NSX manager to AD synchronization will start. Only when it is synchronized properly we should start leveraging **Identity firewall (IDFW)**. This is a one time task and further synchronization is automatic. What next? We can simply create security groups (AD groups) and security policies (Firewall policy) and allow/deny the services based on business requirement. The following diagram shows AD integration with NSX Manager and AD groups MG as source and destination is group of windows machines with http and icmp services allowed between them:

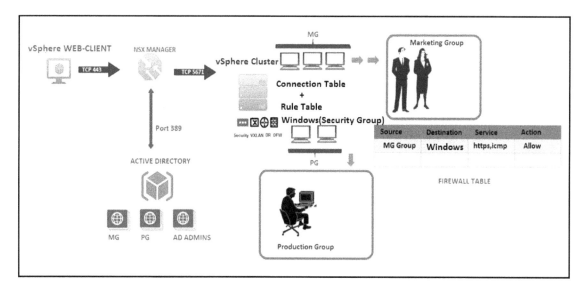

NSX flow monitoring

Network monitoring tools are always difficult to set up, configure, and analyze. To date, most of us will have configured a third-party monitoring tool for analyzing network traffic and taken action accordingly. Maybe we could capture packets at a few points and have them analyzed using Wireshark. Do we really like switching from one management console to another management console for such scenarios? Are we happy with third-party monitoring software and expect all types of integration brilliance to showcase all the traffic? I know most people are not happy with such tools, which are vendor-dependent. We need a tool which will help us analyze things quickly and take proactive action. **NSX flow monitoring** is an built-in feature which gives that visibility and control over any traffic. In a nutshell, it configures Distributed Firewall to capture traffic and we can analyze traffic flow. Flow monitoring data includes the number of sessions and packets transmitted per session. Session details include sources, destinations, applications, and ports being used, and later we can create firewall allow or block rules based on session details. By default, the last 24 hours of data are displayed, the minimum time span is 1 hour and the maximum is 2 weeks.

To enable flow monitoring:

1. Log in to vSphere web client.
2. Select **Networking & Security** from the left navigation pane and then select **Flow Monitoring**.
3. Select the **Configuration** tab.
4. Ensure that **Global Flow Collection Status** is **Enabled** and we are not making any changes with the **Detail Collection Policy**.

The following screenshot depicts **Global Flow Connection Status** set to **Enabled**:

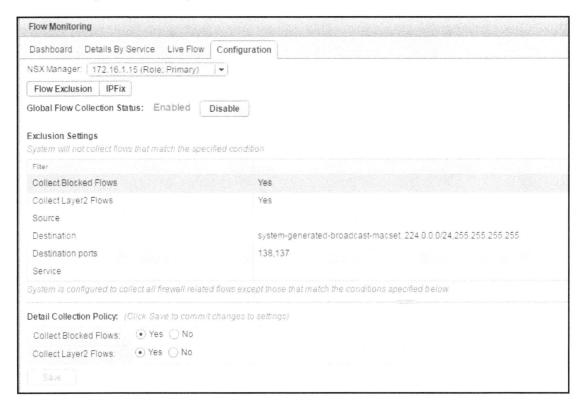

OK! So we have enabled flow monitoring and we should be able to see a few flow stats. In our example, we will quickly check a live flow from a Windows 2008 machine (192.168.2.2).

Capturing a live flow:

1. Log in to vSphere web client.
2. Select **Networking & Security** from the left navigation pane and then select **Flow Monitoring**.
3. Click the **Live Flow** tab.
4. Click **Browse** and select **windows-2008(IPSEC) NIC**.
5. Click **Start** to begin viewing live flow.

The following figure shows live flow stats and I have highlighted a block rule which applies when source windows-2008 192.168.2.2 tries to communicate with destination IP 192.168.4.2:

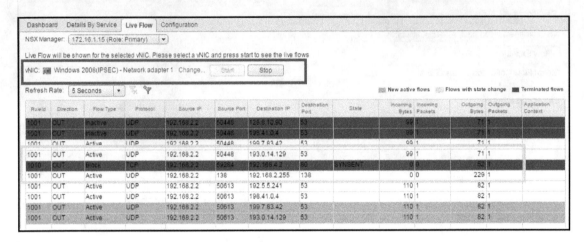

As we can see, this is an excellent feature and we can easily work out not only what type of traffic is allowed and what is blocked but also the incoming and outgoing bytes, which is very important for situations wherein we would like to know which source is sending more bytes or where we are getting more incoming bytes from. In our case, the **TCP-SYNC** packet is sent, but there is no reply since I have created a DFW rule that is blocking the traffic between 192.168.2.2 and 192.168.4.2.

NSX SpoofGuard

Another powerful feature of NSX is SpoofGuard. The SpoofGuard feature will monitor and manage the IP address of a virtual machine. OK! Why do we need such a feature? If a virtual machine is compromised by chance, what are the outcomes? A hacker can certainly change the IP and bypass all firewall policies and the rest will be history. SpoofGuard gives us that granular control to ensure all IP changes are approved, until when traffic would be blocked. NSX Manager will collect the IP address of the virtual machines as long we have a VMware tool installed and running.

The following methods are supported in SpoofGuard:

- **Automatically trust IP assignments on their first use**: This mode allows all traffic from your virtual machines to pass; additionally, it builds a table of vNIC-to-IP address assignments. That way, we can review this table and make IP address changes. Both IPv4 and IPv6 are supported.
- **Manually inspect and approve all IP assignments before use**: This mode blocks all traffic until you approve each vNIC-to-IP address assignment.

That brings us to another question. How about virtual machines which are leveraging DHCP IP? Will they get IP assigned? Do we need to approve them for DHCP IP assignment?

The answer is very simple if we have understood supported SpoofGuard methods. Only in **Manual Inspect**, DHCP traffic won't be allowed until we approve the request; the rule applies the same for DHCP as well. By DHCP will be blocked if we are manually inspecting IP assignment. That being said, let's do a lab test based on the following scenario:

Virtual machines running on the web server logical switch should inspect all IP assignments.

Procedure for SpoofGuard configuration

We need to perform the following steps for SpoofGuard configuration:

1. Firstly, log in to vSphere web client.
2. Click **Networking & Security** and then click **SpoofGuard**.
3. Click the add icon.
4. Type a name for the SpoofGuard policy.
5. We can immediately enable or disable based on business requirements.

6. For **Operation Mode**, we select **Manually inspect and approve all IP assignments before use.** The following screenshot depicts the initial configuration of SpoofGuard:

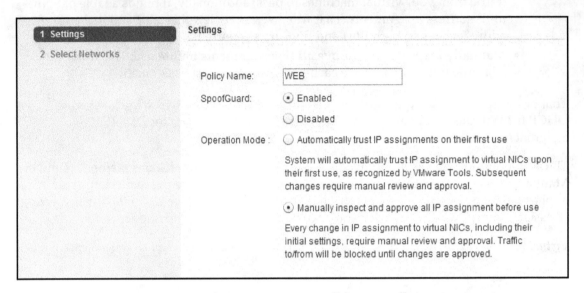

7. To specify where we need to apply the SpoofGuard policy, click **Add** and select the networks, distributed port groups, or logical switches that this policy should apply to. In our example, we are configuring the **Web-Tier** logical switch as shown in the following screenshot:

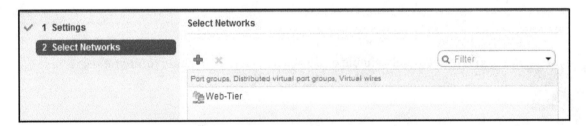

8. Since we have set SpoofGuard to require manual approval of all IP address, let's check that assignment.

In the following screenshot, we are viewing the **Virtual NIC IP Required Approval** screen, IP address changes that require approval before traffic can flow to or from these virtual machines. Other options available are as follows:

- **Active Virtual NICs**
- **Active Virtual NICs Since Last Published**
- **Virtual NICs with Duplicate IP**
- **Inactive Virtual NICs**

Unpublished virtual NICs IP:

To approve an IP address, we need to click **Approve** next to the IP address option. That sums up our detailed discussion on NSX security and monitoring. A few more integrations are certainly possible with NSX, vRealize operations management (previously VROPS) with NSX, vCloud Director integration with NSX; vRealize Automation with NSX , NSX with third-party software such as Palo Alto networks, check point, and so on. Considering the positive momentum NSX has created in the market, more and more integrations will be coming down the line, which makes life easier for all architects. It's definitely worth knowing all these integrations; please read the links I will be providing in `Chapter 8`, *NSX Troubleshooting*. Finally, let's have a quick look at a few key points that need to be taken care of.

Distributed Firewall takeaways

Distributed Firewall is a feature-rich firewall. But we have to be extremely careful while installing and creating rules. Gone are the days when gigantic physical firewalls were used for traffic filtering and other security measures. Applications demanded firewalls to be a little closer to them rather than running at **Top of Rack** (**TOR**). All we needed was a stateful firewall that is more application-aware. When we are inspecting the traffic at near line rate processing that too for East-West traffic which will give us better visibility over the traffic and reduces any attacking loopholes in virtualized data centers, we can call NSX DFW firewall the foundation pillar of **Micro Segmentation**. Worried about bottlenecks? No problem! DFW is the new kid in town. Let's have a quick look at a few key takeaways from this chapter.

DFW doesn't demand any physical network topology changes.

Make a note of all management virtual machines (VMware appliances, third-party appliances, AD, DNS and exchange, and so on) that are installed in the vSphere environment and make a decision about which should be part of DFW protection.

VSphere switch is not supported for policy enforcement; only logical switches and distributed switch port groups are supported. DFW is fully supported with IPv4 and IPv6.

Starting from NSX 6.2, DFW rules leveraging vCenter Server objects even without VMware tools are supported. NSX 6.1 and above has a new option called **reject** in firewall actions. This action is available in NSX Edge as well.

NSX 6.2.3 supports **Trivial File Transfer Protocol** (**TFTP**)-ALG Distributed Firewall rules.

An identity-based firewall is supported only for **Windows Clients**, ideal for East-West data center traffic. However, we can configure it with NSX Edge firewall and a physical firewall, which will bring end-to-end security in the overall data center.

Removing and adding vSphere virtual machines from vCenter won't delete any DFW rules. Make use of the **exclusion list** feature if you want to exclude a VM completely from DFW protection. I will be discussing exclusion lists in more detail in Chapter 8, *NSX Troubleshooting*.

If we are leveraging Identity firewall feature and for some reason there is a synchronization issue between NSX Manager and Active Directory, it will have a direct impact on DFW rules. So this is one scenario wherein Management plane (NSX Manager) outage causing a dataplane traffic issue because firewall is impacted.

If we need to identity applications and allow/block the traffic irrespective of the port and protocols information, best firewall for such use case will be to integrate New generation firewalls like palo alto along with DFW.

It is not mandatory to install the DFW feature in the vSphere management cluster; if we want to install DFW, watch out for the VCenter Server machine. Ensure that the machine is excluded from the list. If there is an other third-party management software running in the same cluster, DFW doesn't have the intelligence to exclude it from protection. I have seen this mistake back in the VCNS days: all of a sudden, VC loses access to all management components. A simple click on the **Install** button will cause a major production outage.

Summary

We started this chapter with an introduction to NSX security and later we covered DFW architecture, use cases, and features. We also had a discussion about monitoring options available in NSX and, finally, we wrapped up the chapter by discussing key points to be noted before installing NSX security features.

In the next chapter, we will discuss cross-VC NSX for a multi-site solution with logical switch, Distributed Logical Router, and DFW installation and configuration across multiple vCenter domains.

7
NSX Cross vCenter

In this chapter, we will have a detailed discussion of the NSX cross vCenter feature. Starting from NSX 6.2, we can manage multiple vCenter Servers from a single pane of glass by leveraging NSX features across vCenter environments. We will primarily cover the following topics:

- Understanding NSX cross vCenter Server
- Components of NSX cross vCenter Server
- Cross vCenter universal logical switches
- Cross vCenter universal logical router
- Network choke points in NSX cross vCenter Server

Understanding NSX cross vCenter Server

Earlier versions of NSX had a **1:1** relationship with vCenter Server and that means NSX features and functionalities were limited to that specific vCenter Server. So whenever we are scaling vCenter Servers, it demands separate installation and configuration of NSX Manager and each of these environments has to be managed separately. When VMware released NSX 6.2 in August 2015, security and cross vCenter Server networking were exciting features that were announced. With cross vCenter networking and security features, we can extend logical switches across vCenter boundaries and, adding to that, we can extend distributed routing and distributed firewalling seamlessly across VCs to provide a true network hybridity between both the sites. There are numerous use cases customers can benefit from with this cross VC NSX integration. The following are a few of them:

- By leveraging cross vCenter Server, we can have a primary and secondary vSphere environment and can easily configure disaster recovery sites.
- Seamless migration of workloads from one vSphere environment to another.

- Simplified data center routing across vCenter Server sites; centralized security policy management; firewall rules can be managed from one centralized location.
- NSX features and functionalities can be locally deployed (single vCenter Server); also we can deploy it across vCenter Server (cross vCenter Server). That way, local objects can be managed locally and global objects can be managed globally.

The following figure depicts a cross vCenter Server NSX environment:

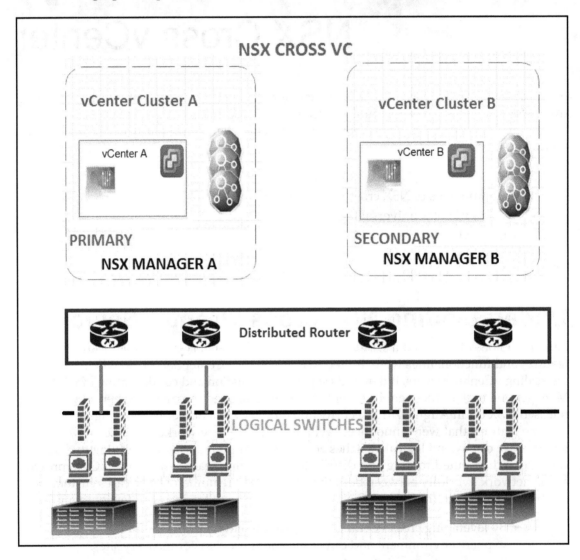

I know we are all excited to know how NSX cross VC works. But let's be very clear with prerequirements and a few points before discussing this feature:

- The VSphere environment should be version 6.0.
- Each vCenter Server should be registered with a unique NSX Manager. Okay! That is an interesting point, isn't it? When I first heard about cross VC NSX architecture, I thought all we needed would be one NSX Manager moving forward. But further reading and lab sessions proved my understanding was wrong.
- We have to promote one NSX Manager as **primary** and the others will be **secondary**.

- We can certainly demote NSX roles based on business requirements. For example, a secondary NSX Manager can be demoted to a standalone NSX Manager and that way, we are going back to where NSX was initially when it started (pre 6.2 NSX version).
- Even though cross VC NSX is a great architecture, I would still call it a new kid in town and it lacks all the features that were possible in a standalone NSX Manager instance. Keeping that negativity aside, I strongly believe newer versions of NSX will start supporting all the features across vCenter Servers.
- Carefully plan and integrate cross VC NSX environments; to be precise, watch out for what features we need in the primary and secondary sites and how we need to manage those features. For example, if we need just a Distributed Firewall feature in the secondary site, I wouldn't recommend cross VC NSX integration unless we want to manage these firewall policies from a single pane of glass.

Components of NSX cross vCenter Server

Cross vCenter NSX includes the following components:

- Universal controller cluster
- Universal transport zone
- Universal logical switch
- Universal distributed logical router
- Universal IP set
- Universal MAC set
- Universal security group

The following table depicts NSX cross vCenter Server deployment options; based on these points, we will have a detailed explanation:

Universal	vCenter A + Primary NSX	vCenter B + Secondary NSX
Controller Cluster	1 Universal Controller Cluster	No Universal Controller Cluster
Transport Zone	1 Universal Transport Zone and Local Transport Zones are Possible	No Universal Transport Zone, Local Transport Zones are possible
Logical Switch	Multiple Universal and Local Logical Switches	Multiple Universal and Local Logical Switches
Distributed Logical Router	Multiple Universal and Local DLR	Multiple Universal and Local DLR
Security Group	Universal Security Groups cannot have dynamic membership or excluded objects. Universal IP sets can include only Universal IP/MAC and Security Groups Local Security Groups are also supported	Universal Security Groups cannot have dynamic membership or excluded objects. Universal IP sets can include only Universal IP/MAC and Security Groups Local Security Groups are also supported

In the preceding table, I have updated key NSX features that customers would be ideally configuring in a cross vCenter NSX environment. Any other features, such as load balancing and L2 bridging, do not have any global level fitting between the NSX sites so they always remain local to the vCenter Server environment. Before exploring universal NSX features, we need to know what roles are available for NSX Manager.

The NSX Manager instance has the following roles and a synchronization module will be running on the primary NSX Manager to ensure universal objects are synchronized to the secondary NSX Manager. The NSX Manager instance has the following roles:

- **Standalone**: Before configuring NSX roles, all the NSX Managers are standalone NSX Managers. A fresh installation of NSX Manager or an upgraded version of NSX Manager from VCNS are perfect examples of standalone NSX Managers.

- **Primary**: There will be only**one Primary NSX Manager** in a cross vCenter NSX environment and we will be creating all universal objects in the primary NSX Manager. To be more specific, any deployment, modification, or deletion tasks will be done on the primary NSX Manager.

- **Secondary**: Whenever a standalone NSX Manager is added to the primary NSX Manager instance, it is called a secondary NSX Manager. All the universal objects are read-only on the secondary NSX Manager instance. A secondary NSX Manager instance cannot have its own controllers. We can have a total of seven secondary NSX Managers.

- **Transit**: There will be instances wherein we need to remove/change primary and secondary roles for the NSX Manager and this is where the transit role is important. However, if the NSX Manager instance has universal objects, it cannot be assigned the standalone role by definition. In such cases, the NSX Manager instance is assigned the transit role. In the transit role, a universal object can only be deleted. An NSX Manager instance can be assigned the secondary role after all the universal objects are deleted.

The following diagram explains the various NSX roles that we have explained so far and the process to promote and demote NSX roles based on universal objects:

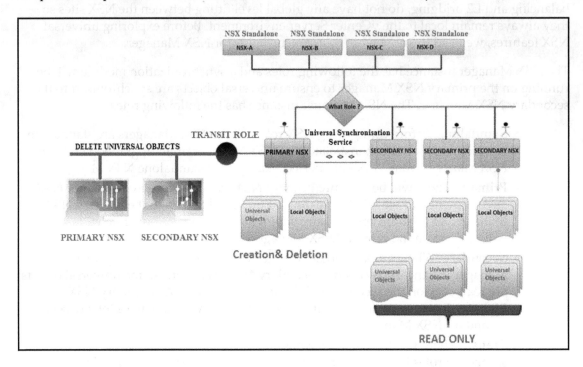

Before moving ahead with further discussion of cross vCenter, we need to know the importance of the **Universal Synchronization Service**. The Universal Synchronization Service is the heart of cross vCenter NSX communication.

Universal Synchronisation Service

The **Universal Synchronization Service** is responsible for synchronizing configuration changes from the primary NSX Manager instance to all the secondary NSX Manager instances. These are inbuilt services that are running in primary NSX Manager and they do REST API calls to secondary NSX Managers for synchronization. Okay, let's do a few quick tests to see what the state of the service is before we start assigning roles to NSX Managers.

The following figure shows a GUI connection to NSX 6.2 and in the highlighted column we can see the NSX Universal Synchronization Service status:

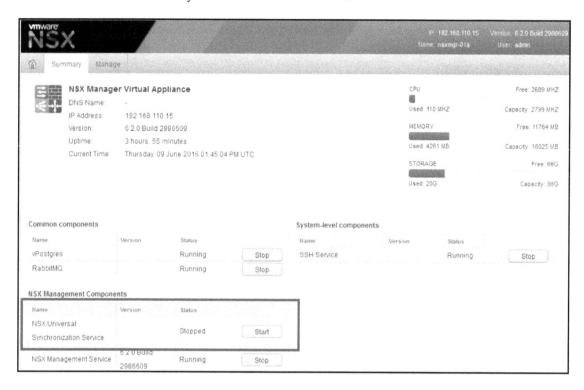

In our setup, we have two NSX Managers and vCenter Servers are registered with a common**Platform Service Controller** (**PSC**). The PSC was introduced in vSphere 6 and handles functions such as vCenter Single Sign-On, licensing, certificate management, and server reservation. Controllers are already deployed in the NSX Manager 192.168.110.15, which will be our primary NSX Manager in a short while. We all know how to register NSX Manager with an individual vCenter Server since we have already discussed that in `Chapter 3`, *NSX Manager Installation and Configuration*. Assuming that we have already done that registration successfully, it's time to promote the **192.168.110.15** NSX Manager as primary and **192.168.210.15** as secondary:

1. Select the **Management** tab and highlight **NSX Manager**s.
2. Select the **Actions** icon.

3. Select **Assign Primary Role**:

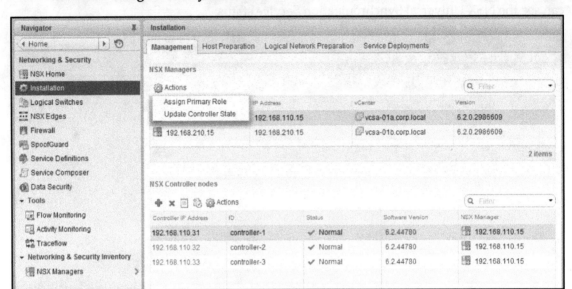

Any guess what will happen when we promote NSX Manager to primary? If your thoughts match the output, I'm going to show that result right away. Congratulations if your answers are correct.

The following figure depicts NSX Manager primary role registration; the **Replicator Service** is automatically starting:

```
2016-06-09 14:06:19.421 GMT  INFO http-nio-127.0.0.1-7441-exec-1 AuditingServiceImpl:147 - [AuditLog] UserName:'corp.local
\administrator', ModuleName:'UniversalSync', Operation:'ASSIGN_PRIMARY_ROLE', Resource:'', Time:'Thu Jun 09 14:06:19.420 GMT
2016', Status:'SUCCESS', Universal Object:'false'
2016-06-09 14:06:15.766 GMT  INFO http-nio-127.0.0.1-7441-exec-1 ReplicatorUtils:52 - Starting Replicator service...
```

The preceding screenshot is the NSX Manager logs from the primary NSX Manager. As we can see in the GUI as well, **Replicator Service** is automatically started since the registration is successful. The following figure shows the Universal Synchronization Service in a running state:

So watch out for this output and verify in the GUI whether the output matches the output in the logs. It is extremely important and useful for troubleshooting.

Universal segment ID

The universal segment ID pool is used to assign VNIs to universal logical switches, to ensure that we don't use the same segment ID pool for local and global logical switches; there would be overlapping segment IDs in that eventually.

The following figure shows **Universal Segment ID pool** creation:

Provide a Segment ID pool and Multicast range unique to this NSX Manager.

Segment ID pool: 5000-5009

(In the range of 5000-16777215)

☐ Enable Multicast addressing

Multicast addresses are required only for Hybrid and Multicast control plane modes.

▼ Universal Segment ID pool and Multicast range

Provide a Universal Segment ID pool and Multicast range unique to this NSX Manager.

Universal Segment ID pool: 200000-202000

(In the range of 5000-16777215)

☐ Enable Universal Multicast addressing

Universal Multicast addresses are required only for Hybrid and Multicast control plane modes.

OK   Cancel

The whole purpose of creating universal logical switches is to span the logical network across vCenter sites without doing traditional complex routing and switching. That way, universal logical switches will be available on all the vCenter Servers in the cross domain NSX site and we can simply connect virtual machines to those logical switches. The virtual machine logical switches will always remain as port groups and NSX will take care of cross vCenter switching. Haven't we configured a more simplified Layer 2 switching than this? First of all, was it possible do a Layer 2 switching like this in the past? I strongly believe we have all already moved away from legacy network design thinking with the amount of awareness that we have added so far in this book.

Let's go ahead and add a secondary role to our second NSX Manager so that we can start creating universal transport zones and universal logical switches.

The procedure for adding a secondary NSX Manager is as follows:

1. Log in to the vCenter linked to the primary NSX Manager.
2. Navigate to **Home** | **Networking & Security** | **Installation** and select the **Management** tab.
3. Click the primary NSX Manager. Then select **Actions** | **Add Secondary NSX Manager**.
4. Enter the IP address, username, and password of the secondary NSX Manager.
5. Click **OK**.

The following figure depicts the **Add Secondary NSX Manager** option:

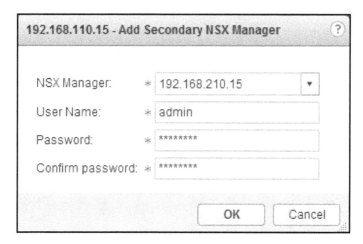

A successful addition of a secondary NSX Manager will show the role as secondary as depicted in the following screenshot:

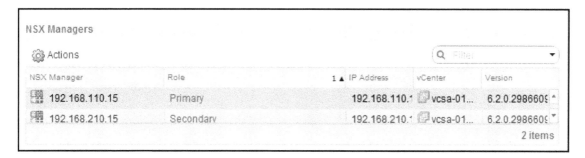

Universal transport zone

Since we have a primary and secondary NSX Manager, let's go ahead and create a universal transport zone. First and foremost, there can only be **one universal transport zone in a cross vCenter NSX environment**. During the NSX Manager roles in this chapter, we have gone through the difference between primary, secondary and transit roles and there is no exception while creating a universal transport zone. Universal objects are always created from the primary NSX Manager.

The following figure shows universal logical switch creation and we have added a primary NSX-VC pairing vSphere cluster:

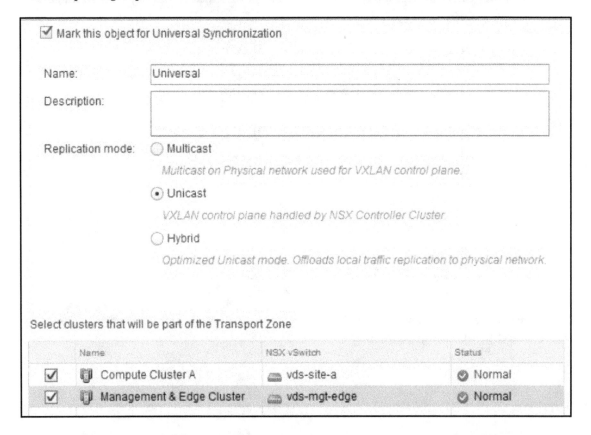

To add clusters from the secondary NSX-VC pairing vSphere site, we need to change the manager settings to secondary and click on **Connect Cluster Option**, which will display all clusters in the secondary NSX-VC site. Whenever we add new clusters, all we need to do is connect those newly added clusters to the universal transport zone and in my view this is the simplest way we can scale a software-defined data center:

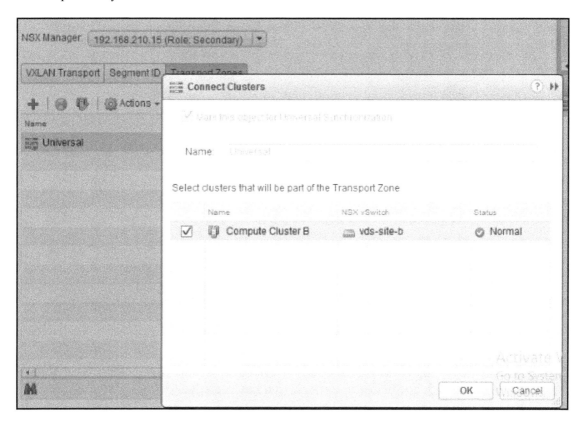

Let's do a quick test: we will go ahead and create a universal logical switch and will check if logical switches are getting populated in the primary and secondary NSX sites. Sounds great? Let's get started then.

Cross vCenter universal logical switch creation

Okay! We need to check a few prerequirements for logical switch creation to ensure that we are able to create the logical switch at the same time and it is functioning as expected. The following are the key points that should be followed while creating a universal logical switch:

- A VSphere distributed switch should be configured
- Controllers must be deployed in the primary NSX Manager
- VSphere Host clusters must be prepared for NSX
- VXLAN must be configured
- A universal segment ID pool must be configured (should not overlap with local segment ID)
- A universal transport zone must be created

Let's go ahead and create a **universal logical switch**:

1. In vSphere web client, navigate to **Home** | **Networking & Security** | **Logical Switches**.
2. Select the NSX Manager on which you want to create a logical switch (this should be the primary NSX Manager; if we select the secondary NSX Manager, it won't be universal object selection).
3. Click the **New Logical Switch** icon.

This being a universal logical switch, we certainly need to have a universal transport zone and segment ID created; however, we have created that already. Assuming that we have met all the pre requirements, let's move on:

1. Type the universal logical switch name; in our example, we are naming it **Universal** switch.
2. Select the **Transport Zone**; this should be the **Universal Transport Zone** created earlier in this chapter.

The following figure represents universal logical switch creation:

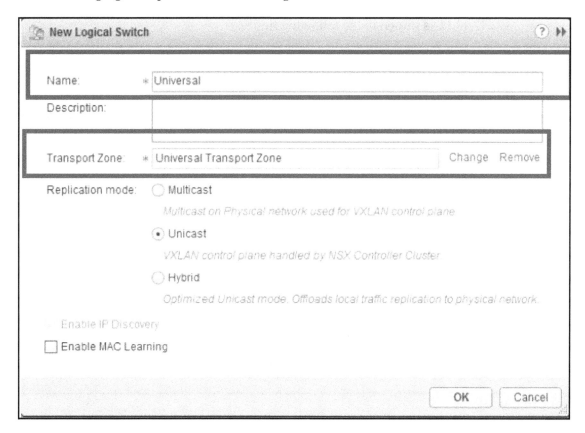

Adding virtual machines to universal logical switches

Since we have already created universal logical switches, we will go ahead and attach two virtual machines from two vCenter sites and perform a basic ping test. Considering the amount of knowledge that we have added so far, this lab task will be a cakewalk for all of us. Let's get started:

1. In logical switches, we need to select the logical switch to which you want to add virtual machines.
2. Click the **Add Virtual Machine** icon.

3. Select the virtual machines you want to add to the logical switch. In our case, we are selecting the **Web-Site A** machine, which is preconfigured with IP **172.17.10.11** as shown in the following figure:

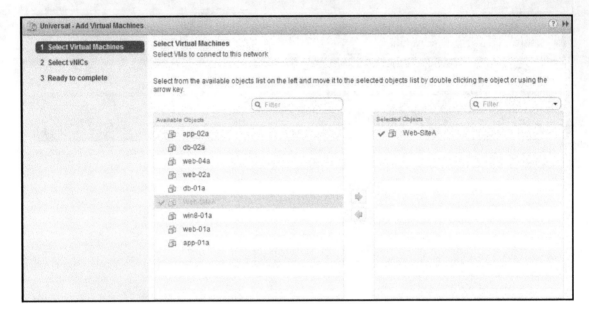

4. Select the vNICs that you want to connect as shown in the following figure:

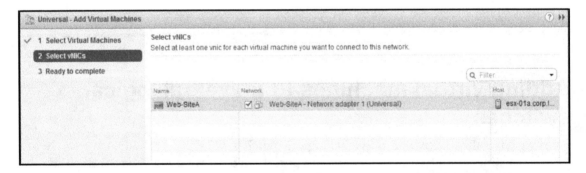

5. Click **Next** and **Finish** the connection configuration task for **Web-Site A.**

The following screenshot portrays the Web-Site A machine and its IP details:

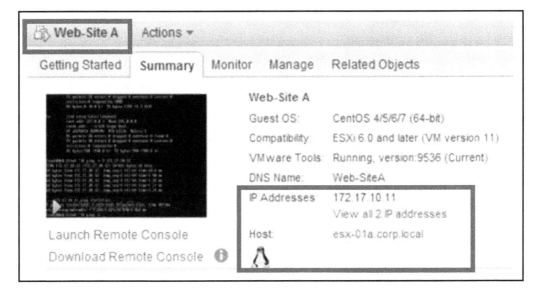

> If we don't see the correct virtual machine in the available objects section, there's a strong chance we are in the wrong NSX Manager. We have to be in the correct NSX Manager (primary/secondary) to see the VC-virtual machine inventory list.

6. Since we have done with the Site-A, virtual machines have been added to the universal logical switch, we need to switch our NSX Manager role to secondary so that we can add machines from the secondary NSX Manager VC inventory to the same universal logical switch. How do we do that? It's a simple switch and is demonstrated in the following screenshot:

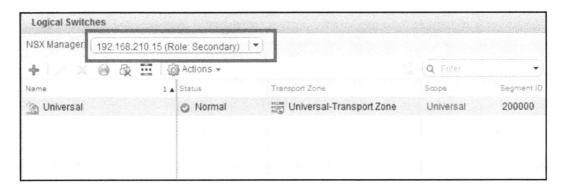

7. We need to repeat Steps 1,2, and 3 and add virtual machine **Web-Site B** from the second vCenter Server, which is preconfigured with IP **172.17.10.12**.

8. Click the **Add Virtual Machine** icon.

9. Select the virtual machines you want to add to the logical switch. In our case, we are selecting the **Web-Site B** machine.

The following screenshot shows the **Web-Site B** machine and its IP details:

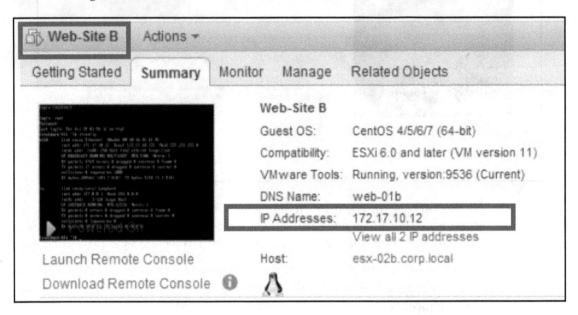

Now we have created a universal logical switch and connected the **Web-Site A** and **Web-Site B** machines residing in two vCenter Servers. Traditionally, we need a Layer 2 switch for such circumstances since virtual machines are on two vCenter Servers and the same subnet. However, the cross vCenter NSX universal logical switch is a game-changer for data center Layer 2 switching. This is certainly a great use case not only for cross vCenter virtual machine connectivity we can easily design an active-active,active-passive vSphere data center for disaster recovery configuration with VMware SRM.

Let's do a simple ping test to confirm if these web servers are communicating as expected. The following screenshot shows **Web-Site B** virtual machine connectivity from **Web-Site A**:

```
[root@Web-SiteA ~]# ping -c 5 172.17.10.12
PING 172.17.10.12 (172.17.10.12) 56(84) bytes of data.
64 bytes from 172.17.10.12: icmp_seq=1 ttl=64 time=10.8 ms
64 bytes from 172.17.10.12: icmp_seq=2 ttl=64 time=1.50 ms
64 bytes from 172.17.10.12: icmp_seq=3 ttl=64 time=1.28 ms
64 bytes from 172.17.10.12: icmp_seq=4 ttl=64 time=1.51 ms
64 bytes from 172.17.10.12: icmp_seq=5 ttl=64 time=3.24 ms
```

Okay! So we have Layer 2 connectivity between two vCenter sites by leveraging universal logical switches. If this entire network flow sounds complex or confusing, let's focus on the following figure, which portrays the entire configuration that we did so far for establishing universal logical switching:

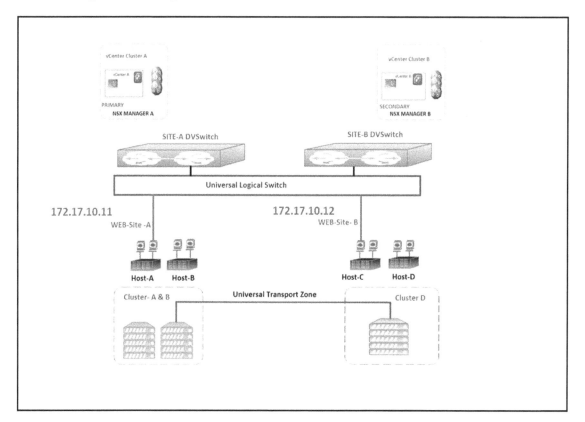

Cross vCenter Server Universal Logical Routers

Universal Logical Routers provides a optimized routing between vCenter Server sites for East-West data center traffic. For now, we can call this router a **Global NSX Router**, which will ease management tasks such as configuring and creating routes (static/dynamic) and firewall rules from a single pane of glass. Once again, I will re-emphasize: creation/deletion and all management activity relative to universal logical routers can be only done from the primary NSX Manager. We will go ahead and configure a cross vCenter Server universal logical router and establish a routing between two vCenter Server sites. We are taking the same virtual machines that we used in universal logical switching for this configuration; however, I have changed the IP/subnet of **Web-Site B**, which demands a routing between **Web-Site A** and **Web-Site B**. Let's get started then:

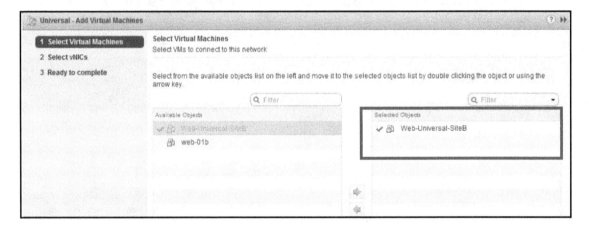

The procedure for deploying a universal logical router is as follows:

1. Log in to vSphere web client.
2. Click on **Networking & Security** and then click **NSX Edges**.

3. Select **Universal Logical (Distributed) Router** (we will discuss local egress in the *Network choke points* section of this chapter):

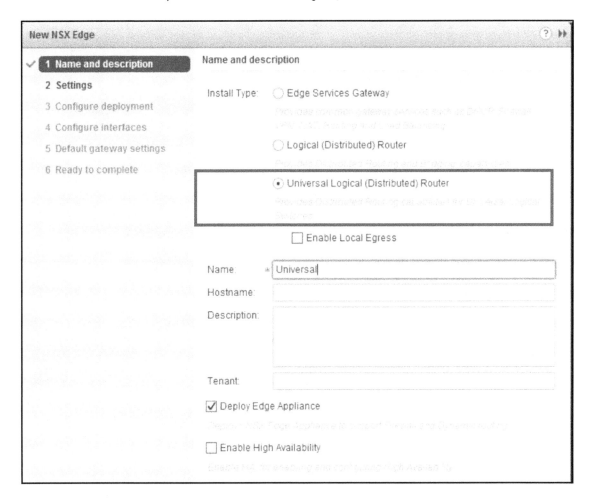

4. Enter the **User Name** and P**assword** for the **Universal Distributed Logical Router (UDLR)** as shown in the following figure:

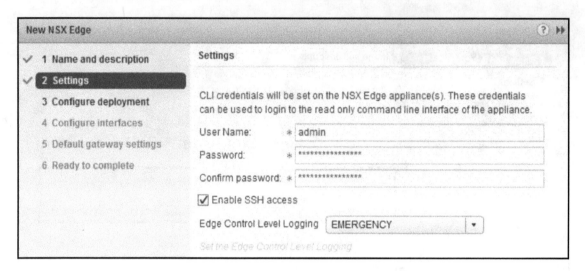

5. Select the **Datacenter** and **NSX EdgeAppliance** details as shown in the following screenshot:

Please note that **NSX Edge Appliance** is not mandatory if we are leveraging only static routes. However, **Appliance deployment** is a must for dynamic routing and firewall.

6. For High Availability interface configuration, we connect the interface to the vSphere distributed port group and they will communicate over the APIPA range (169.250.0.0/26) IP address as shown in the following screenshot:

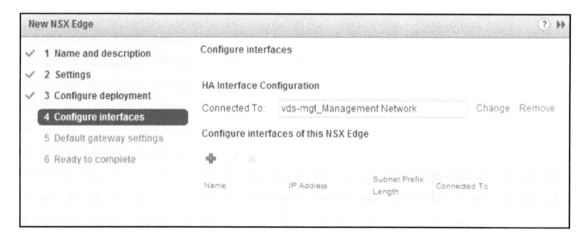

7. Finally, we will add logical interfaces to the UDLR.

   The following screenshot shows the universal switch connection from Site-A to connect the Web-Site-A VM to the UDLR:

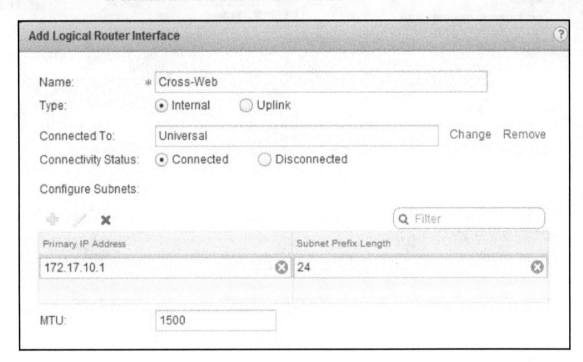

8. We need to repeat Step 7 to add the Web-Site-B (VM residing in the second vCenter) to the UDLR as shown in the following screenshot:

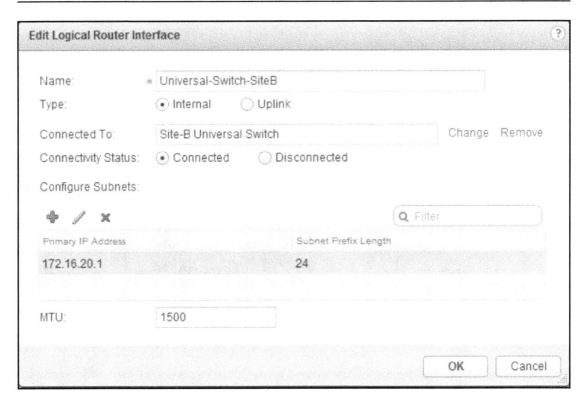

Now that we have connected both the universal switches to the UDLR, let's go ahead and verify the routing table. No rocket science here, if we have followed all the steps so far diligently. Our UDLR should show those two logical networks as directly connected networks. The following screenshot depicts the output for the following command:

```
Net-vdr -route -l UDLR-ID
```

```
[root@esx-01a:~] net-vdr --route -l default+edge-941a1ead-a31a-4c58-8bf5-704611b2173a

VDR default+edge-941a1ead-a31a-4c58-8bf5-704611b2173a Route Table
Legend: [U: Up], [G: Gateway], [C: Connected], [I: Interface]
Legend: [H: Host], [F: Soft Flush] [!: Reject] [E: ECMP]

Destination      GenMask          Gateway        Flags     Ref Origin  UpTime    Interface
-----------      -------          -------        -----     --- ------  ------    ---------
172.16.20.0      255.255.255.0    0.0.0.0        UCI       3   MANUAL  3885      30d400000000b
172.17.10.0      255.255.255.0    0.0.0.0        UCI       1   MANUAL  6631      30d400000000a
```

Since the UDLR is showing **172.16.20.0** and **172.17.10.0** networks connected, we should be able to perform a simpleICMP ping between these machines, considering we have appropriate firewall rules added in the router. In our example, the default rule is to allow all the traffic so there should not be any choke points here.

The following screenshot portrays a successful ICMP ping from **Web-Site-B** (172.16.10.11) to **Web-Site-A** (172.17.10.11):

```
Web-Site-B

64 bytes from 172.17.10.11: icmp_seq=16 ttl=63 time=2.86 ms
64 bytes from 172.17.10.11: icmp_seq=16 ttl=63 time=2.88 ms
64 bytes from 172.17.10.11: icmp_seq=17 ttl=63 time=1.34 ms
64 bytes from 172.17.10.11: icmp_seq=17 ttl=63 time=1.48 ms
64 bytes from 172.17.10.11: icmp_seq=18 ttl=63 time=1.14 ms
64 bytes from 172.17.10.11: icmp_seq=18 ttl=63 time=1.20 ms
64 bytes from 172.17.10.11: icmp_seq=19 ttl=63 time=2.70 ms
```

Let's take an example, to be clear with the overall learning process, showing how routes are getting pushed to the underlying ESXi host; we have a multi-tenant topology as an example which I have shown in the following figure:

1. Dynamic routing protocol (OSPF) is running between Site-A and B Edges to their respective data center routers.
2. Site-A and Site-B NSX Edges are connected with Universal Distributed Logical Routers.
3. Static routes are created on NSX Edges to reach the 172.16.10.0 series network (we can certainly leverage dynamic routing protocols as well, based on business requirements).
4. UDLR control VMs will send the learnt route to the NSX Controller cluster for distribution. Just to reiterate, controllers are running only in the primary NSX Manager since there is a cross VC NSX solution and all NSX Managers are well aware of universal NSX objects through the universal synchronization service.
5. The primary NSX Controllers will send those routes to the underlying ESXi hosts.

6. The ESXi host kernel routing module will update its routing table and will take care of data path traffic for those networks which it has learnt from the controllers.

7. The preceding mentioned six steps are basic routing learning processes in an NSX environment:

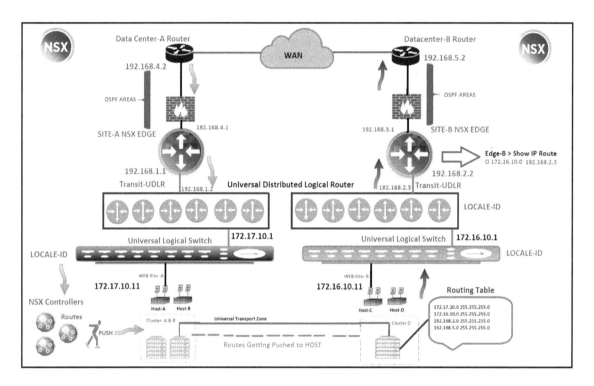

Network choke points

Let me get started by saying: *Never offer or implement any design unless you are well aware that it addresses all the customer's needs.*

That rule is not specific to marketing or sales folk. It's general advice for anyone who deals with technology. If not, we will hear the feedback: *I'm having a nightmare; all the problems started happening after that design change. Can you please get rid of that?* We have designed or seen various types of vSphere networks. Every network topology will have a loophole. Nothing is perfect in this world and all we can do is ensure that we are better prepared for failures, this seems more like an advantage than a failure? I want all of you to pause for a minute and have a look at the preceding topology; make a note of all failure scenarios that might interrupt data traffic. Adding to that, if we have carefully observed the topology, we will see that universal control VMs and Edges are running on two different sites. So how will the UDLR control VM ensure that whatever routes it is learning from that specific NSX Edge are the only routes learnt by the underlying ESXi host that are specific to that site? I know that is a slightly confusing statement. Never mind, all we need is that routes learned by Site-A appliances (Edges/Control VM) are sent to the Site-A ESXi host and vice versa for Site-B. Okay! Let's get started then and keep reading the following useful points to ensure that our design satisfies our customer requirement without inviting any further problems:

1. Both the data centers have two NSX appliances running and we need to ensure they are running in HA mode with vSphere HA also configured. That way, single appliance/host failure will have less impact:
   - NSX Edge
   - UDLR Control VM

2. Ensure that we are using**LOCALE-ID (by default, this value is set to the NSX Managers-UUID)**. With the Locale-ID configuration, NSX Controllers will send routes to ESXi hosts matching Locale-ID. Going via our topology, each site ESXi host will maintain a site-specific local routing table. We can set Locale-ID per cluster, host level and UDLR level. This would perfectly fit in a multi-tenant network/cloud environment wherein each tenant wants to maintain routes which are specific to that tenant.

3. All **South-North** traffic is handled by **Site A NSX Edge** and **SITE B NSX Edge** in their respective sites. Starting from NSX 6.1, **Equal Cost Multi Path** (**ECMP**) is supported. Hence, we can deploy multiple NSX Edges and the ECMP algorithm will HASH the traffic based on source and destination IP. ECMP can be enabled on Edges and DLR. That way, if there is a failure, it will recalculate the HASH and will route the traffic to the active edge/DLR. In addition to that, there will be designs that might demand back-to-back ECMP configuration, Distributed Logical Router to NSX Edge and NSX Edge to physical routers.

4. We should never design something that breaks a working topology. While we deal with ECMP, we need to be aware that NSX Edge has a stateful firewall. There is a good chance we might have asymmetric routing issues; basically, a packet that travels from source to destination uses one path and while replying, takes another path, because at any time only one Edge will be aware of the traffic flow. No worries: while we enable ECMP in NSX 6.1, we will get a message that says enabling this feature will **disable Edge firewall**. **Don't worry**, we are not compromising on firewall rules in such designs. Either we can deploy any third-party physical firewall (as shown in the figure) between NSX Edges and Upstream router or we need to leverage Distributed Firewall, which will filter the traffic at the VNIC level. However, starting from NSX 6.1.3, ECMP and logical firewall can work together and for the same reason it won't get disabled by default when we enable ECMP. However, starting from NSX 6.1.3, ECMP and logical firewall can work together and for the same reason it won't get disabled by default when we enable ECMP (Active/Standby NSX Edges). The following diagram depicts an **ECMP**-added configuration for the same topology:

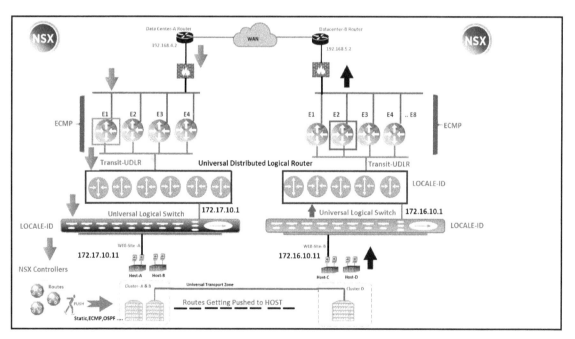

5. Since we have NSX Edges running on each site, **overlapping** IP addresses are supported by configuring a NAT on the site-specific Edge. Again, a highly demanding use case, especially for cloud providers.

6. We can have eight NSX Edges participating in ECMP configuration at a time; in our case, eight ECMP edges per site with a total of 16 Edges we can run in that way.

7. How about a worst case scenario of complete Site A or Site B failure one at a time? There is certainly a solution for any problem, but in this case, the solution will be slightly tedious and based on the physical network design. Reconfiguring all NSX components in another site may not work.

8. Site-B is where we have the primary NSX Manager and Site-B had a complete failure. Starting from NSX Manager role changing, we need to deploy Edges and appliances and can bring the environment back to normal only if the physical network design is equally matching for both the sites. I know this is a tedious process,so if we want to automate such tasks,we need to leverage NSX API and VRO workflow's so that that would ease lot of manual tasks. In a rare case, we may have to reconfigure the physical network so that Site-B machines can communicate with the physical network while they are residing in Site-A during the outage.

There is a lot to be discussed about types of failures, such as NSX components in network sites failing at the same time or virtual environment and physical network partial/full failure scenarios. There are also routing protocol (OSPF/BGP) specific failure scenarios that also bring up some good points for discussion. It is extremely hard to cover all such failure scenarios and carry out precautionary steps based on the type of design in just one book. Luckily, the NSX product documentation from VMware is not limited to installation, configuration, and general designs. There are a few design guides they have released specific to vendor integration, such as NSX+UCS design, NSX+CISCO ACI, and so on. It's worth reading such documents once we have mastered the basics and, hopefully, what we have learnt so far in all seven chapters is a foundation step for climbing the network virtualization ladder. It's been a remarkable discussion so far on VMware NSX topologies and, optimistically, by this time, we all are clear on how VMware NSX is reinventing data center networking.

Summary

We started this chapter with an introduction to NSX cross vCenter Server followed by cross vCenter Server components, and universal object creation, and we ended by discussing a few design decisions that we should be well aware of during cross vCenter Server NSX deployment. Way back, network troubleshooting was single-handedly done by network architects and support engineers, which made life easy for vSphere folk. NSX being a network software layer running on top of vSphere, people often believe that it might make their life somewhat threatening since they have a clear visibility on both for both hypervisor and network virtualization layers.

For me, troubleshooting is an art; if we follow a systematic procedure for checking a problem, resolving the problem is a cakewalk. There is no secret or straightforward automation that will help us analyze and fix a problem in network virtualization.

In the next chapter, we will have a detailed discussion on NSX troubleshooting. So let's ensure that we recall whatever we learnt and get our hands dirty by applying those points based on the situation.

8

NSX Troubleshooting

Let me start this chapter with a famous quote from Antisthenes:

"Not to unlearn what you have learned is the most necessary kind of learning"

I couldn't find a better quote than that for giving everyone a heads-up on how vital it is to ensure that we recollect what we have learned so far in previous chapters about how to approach a problem to see what the best solution is. For the best solution to also be the quickest, we truly need to know how to approach a scenario, where to start looking, what logs are useful, and lastly, when to engage the vendor for further troubleshooting. As we all know, our course is focused on NSX with vSphere. NSX is tightly integrated with vSphere.

Taking a real example, even a well-constructed building will not stand on a weak foundation. A bad vSphere design will have a direct impact on NSX components, no matter how good the NSX design is. This rule of thumb is the same for any VMware solution that runs on top of vSphere. In this chapter, we will cover the following topics:

- NSX installation and registration issues
- The log collection process and steps
- VXLAN troubleshooting

NSX Manager installation and registration issues

Installing NSX Manager is one of the easiest tasks, and the bitter truth is that anyone who is familiar with vSphere OVA/OVF deployment can easily deploy an NSX Manager without any prior knowledge of NSX products. We know for sure, that in a production environment, no one will follow that method. However, I still want to educate you all about the importance of NSX installation. Let's carefully go through the following points:

- There should not be any vCloud networking security (VCNS/vShield Manager) registered with the same vCenter when we are trying to register NSX Manager. If we find any such environments, we must ensure that we are unregistering one of the solutions—definitely VCNS/vShield, since that is an outdated solution compared with NSX Manager. That doesn't mean we can have two NSX Managers registered with the same vCenter Server. However, we can upgrade VCNS to NSX and I will be sharing the upgrade guide link in the chapter's final section.

- Never import any previously used NSX Manager instance to a new environment and register it as a solution with a new vCenter.

- Always check if NSX Manager is registered with how many vSphere solutions. For example, we might have a **vCloudAutomation Center** (**VCAC**) and **vCloud Director** (**VCD**) registered with NSX Manager A, which is also registered with a vCenter Server environment. The reason why I'm more curious about such solutions is that careful planning and design is required not only for installation but also for uninstallation of NSX products during break fix time. Each solution's integration demands separate steps while unregistering NSX Manager.

- Always take a backup of NSX Manager after initial deployment of the software. Never depend on the vSphere snapshot feature for this backup activity.

- NSX Manager can be treated as a normal vSphere virtual machine for troubleshooting any network-related issues. For example, we can migrate NSX Manager from one host to another host, or check the ESXTOP command to know Tx and Rx counts for isolating a network issue.

- While registering with vCenter Server, we have two options:

- **Lookup service registration**: Lookup service registration is an optional feature for importing SSO users. However, if we are integrating with an SSO identity source, we need to follow all vendor-specific best practices for identity source availability. But, it's worth remembering that if SSO is down except for login to NSX Manager, it won't have any impact on NSX components and their features.

- **vCenter Server Registration**: vCenter Server registration is the first and most critical integration. Hence, we need to ensure that we have proper connectivity and configuration for the following points:

  - DNS resolution should be configured between **NSX Manager** and **vCenter Server**.

  - **NTP** should be configured properly; this point might be very familiar for most of the experts, but I will still reiterate it: The impact of wrong NTP is very high when we integrate the lookup service (SSO) and try to leverage SSO-based authentication.

  - **Firewall** ports should be opened between NSX Manager and vCenter Server. Always verify VMware **Knowledge Base** (**KB**) article for port requirements. The following link leads to a VMware KB article, which talks about all the port requirements:

    - `https://kb.vmware.com/selfserv ice/search.do?cmd=displayKC&do cType=kc&docTypeID=DT_KB_1_1&e xternalId=2079386`

    - Ensure that we are using vCenter Server administrative user rights while registering with NSX Manager. We can certainly use the `administrator@vsphere.local` account to register NSX with vCenter, vCloud Director, and vRealize Automation products.

Troubleshooting NSX Manager

Based on the situation, we may have to collect diagnostic information for NSX Manager for VMware Support. Keep the following steps handy for such scenarios.

Collecting NSX Manager logs via GUI

The steps to collect NSX Manager logs via GUI are as follows:

1. Log in to the **NSX Manager** virtual appliance through a web browser.
2. In **NSX Manager Virtual Appliance Management**, click **Download Tech Support Log**.
3. Click **Download** | **Save**. The following screenshot depicts the NSX Manager logs download:

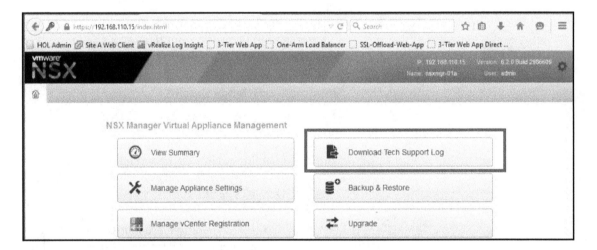

Collecting NSX Manager logs via CLI

There might be instances when the NSX Manager GUI is not working and we might need to depend on the CLI for collecting logs. For CLI haters, there is no escape this time; we need to go through the following steps to capture NSX Manager logs:

1. Log in to the **NSX Manager** virtual appliance through a SSH session.
2. Go to **Enable Mode**, by typing `enable`.

3. Issue the following command in **Enable Mode**, which will save the NSX Manager logs in a remote location based on the host name that we selected:

```
export tech-support scp USERNAME@HOSTNAME:FILENAME
```

The following screenshot illustrates NSX CLI log capturing:

```
                                    192.168.110.15 - PuTTY
login as: admin
admin@192.168.110.15's password:
nsxmgr-01a> enable
Password:
nsxmgr-01a# export tech-support scp root@linux:nsxmanager
Preparing data to export...
done
Exporting...
```

VMware Installation Bundle

Hypervisors are basically the backbone of network virtualization. Virtual machines are able to leverage NSX features primarily because the ESXi host is a network-virtualized host. One of the most critical pillars of an NSX installation is ESXi host preparation. If we don't have the right modules running in the ESXi host, the whole purpose of leveraging NSX features will be defeated. Symptoms would be that we might not be able to install feature *X*, or we can configure feature *X*, but the functionality is impacted. Watch out for the following VIBs in the ESXi host:

- esx-vxlan
- esx-vsip
- esx-dvfilter-switch-security (starting from NSX 6.2.0, esx-dvfilter-switch-security is part of esx-vxlan vibs)

This is the command to check if VIB is installed in ESXi host:

```
esxcli software vib list | grep vibname
```

Since these are VIBs, we can manually uninstall and install the same during break fix scenarios. But the real question is, who is pushing these VIBs? That's where I have seen the majority of issues. Behind the scenes, vCenter Server ESX Agent Managers (**EAM**) are responsible for installing these VIBs. So, first and foremost, the EAM service should be up and running. The following steps are useful for collecting EAM based upon the operating system and vCenter Server flavor.

EAM log location

Following are the EAM log locations for respective vCenter Server and operating system versions:

- VMware vSphere 5.1.x/5.5.x (EAM is a part of the common Tomcat server):
    - Windows 2003: `C:\Documents and Settings\All Users\Application Data\VMware\VMware VirtualCenter\Logs\eam.log`
    - Windows 2008: Same as Windows 2003, the VC log directory is located at `C:\ProgramData\VMware\VMware VirtualCenter\Logs\`
    - **vCenter Server Virtual Appliance (VCVA)**: `/storage/log/vmware/vpx/eam.log`
- VMware vSphere 6.x (EAM is a standalone service and has embedded tcserver):
    - Windows 2003: `C:\Documents and Settings\All Users\Application Data\VMware\CIS\logs\eam\eam.log`
    - Windows 2008: Same as Windows 2003, the VC log directory is located at `C:\ProgramData\VMware\VMware VirtualCenter\Logs\`
    - CloudVM: `/storage/log/vmware/eam/eam.log`

I have seen a lot of issues, especially when a vCenter Server installation is a Windows-based installation, with EAM trying to use port 80 for downloading VIBs. At times, we might have other applications or services running in VC, which might be leveraging port 80 and will cause VIB download failures, so we have to change the default EAM ports. However, starting from VMware vSphere 6.0, VIB downloads over port 443 (instead of port 80) are supported. This port is opened and closed dynamically. The intermediate devices (firewalls) between the ESXi hosts and vCenter Server must allow traffic using this port. With that, we will move on to our next topic: control plane and data plane log collection.

Control plane and data plane log collection

Log collection is vital for proactive and root cause analysis. How many times have we ended up collecting the wrong set of logs or received feedback that we have to enable or increase certain logging levels to ensure that we have the right set of logs to analyze the root cause? Technically, that type of feedback is digestible. However, when it comes to production impact, it would be a disappointment to find that there is nothing conclusive, even after going through the logs. There is only one solution for this issue: we should know what logs need to be collected and most importantly, from which locality. First and foremost, we need to get some background knowledge on the following points:

Understanding the physical topology

Understanding the physical topology is not only important for overall NSX design and feature configuration, it is equally important to share effective feedback if there is a better way to approach the overall design. The following mentioned points are something that we need to keep handy:

- Physical Network design – Spine-leaf/layer2 architecture
- Existing firewall deployments and rules
- Overall datacenter Routing and Switching topology
- vSphere cluster design (placement in racks) and topology. In addition to that, how many clusters (single-site, multi-site), data centers and active-active or active-passive physical data center designs required currently or future configuration.
- vSphere distributed Switch Uplink policy

The following are some recommendations based on the preceding points:

- **Physical Network design – Spine-leaf/layer2 architecture**: Spine/Leaf architecture is the best and most widely used connectivity now a days because of full mesh connectivity, less latency, high bandwidth, ECMP routing and most importantly easy expansion of network is achievable.
- **Existing firewall deployments and rules**: This is an important check primarily because of NSX Edge Firewall and Microsegmentation capabilities. My suggestion would be try to integrate vRealize Network-insight software to understand overall traffic growth in North-South and East-West direction and then decide what firewall policies to be configured at which points. In the closing section of the chapter i have given a small summary on vRealize Network-insight software.

- **Overall datacenter routing and switching topology**:
    - Here we are mainly focusing on routing protocols used in physical network – for example OSPF, BGP, ISIS.
    - For example based on the AREA types configured for OSPF, assuming that upstream router is **Area Border Router (ABR)** we need to know what routes should be injected to Upstream router from NSX Edge and appropriate firewall policies for allowing the traffic.
    - In the Layer 2 side ideally ESXI, VXLAN traffic is the most important parameters that we need to know for assigning/configuring VLAN-ID (Management, VMotion, Storage, VXLAN).
- **vSphere cluster design (placement in racks) and topology**:
    - Cluster design should ideally be Management & Edge Cluster Separated from Compute Cluster with minimum of 4 Host in Management & Edge Cluster and maximum of 64 host in Computer Cluster (only if environment is running vSphere 6.0)
    - For disaster recovery environment configured with SRM and NSX.It is recommended to maintain similar physical and virtual design in the DR site. Situations might demand workloads to be running in DR site for long time, hence we need to follow that strict rule.
- **vSphere distributed Switch Uplink policy**: This is the same topic that we have discussed in Chapter 3, *NSX Manager Installation and Configuration*:
    - Here we need to select and configure NIC teaming and failover policies. For example if we choose LACP configuration, we are limited with Single VTEP configuration, however route based on port and source MAC hash support multi VTEP configuration. Prevention is better that cure, it is recommended to load balance VXLAN traffic across all available uplinks rather than inviting performance issues.

The idea behind these minor point discussion is to ensure all configurations/design aspects are taken care well in advance rather than spending time later to do configuration and performance tweaking.

NSX Controller log collection

Controller is the real game changer component in the overall architecture of NSX. For the same reason, it remains a critical piece when it comes to troubleshooting. As we all know, controllers are deployed from NSX Manager in an **Open Virtualization Appliance** (**OVA**). In a worst-case scenario, even the deployment of controllers might fail, and that would be a showstopper for any NSX implementation. The majority of such failures happen for the following two reasons:

- DNS
- NTP

There should be proper DNS/NTP configuration between ESXi hosts, vCenter Server, and NSX Manager for a successful deployment of NSX Controller. Apart from this point, a successful deployment of any virtual machine in vSphere certainly needs enough compute and storage capacity, and NSX Controller is no exception, primarily because these are virtual machines from an ESXi host perspective. For collecting NSX Controller logs, we need to complete the following steps:

1. Firstly, we need to log in to vCenter Server using the vSphere web client.
2. Click on **Networking and Security**.
3. Click **Installation** on the left-hand pane.
4. Under the **Manage** tab, select the controller you want to download logs from.
5. Click **Download Tech support logs**.
6. The following screenshot depicts the NSX Controller log collection process:

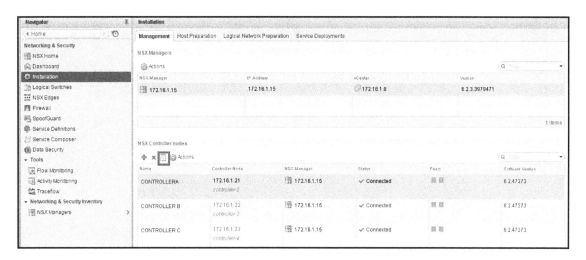

How about if the web client is down, or we don't have access to the web client? What method we can follow to collect the logs? There are two options in those cases:

1. Using a vSphere client session, we can connect to vCenter Server or the ESXi host where the controller is running, and we can take a VM console session to controller to leverage the CLI command for log collection.
2. Take an SSH session directly to controller and execute a CLI command for log collection.

Collecting NSX Controller logs using CLI steps

Firstly, log into the NSX Controller for which you want to gather logs using any of the previous steps, and execute the following command, as shown in the screenshot:

```
save status-report filename
```

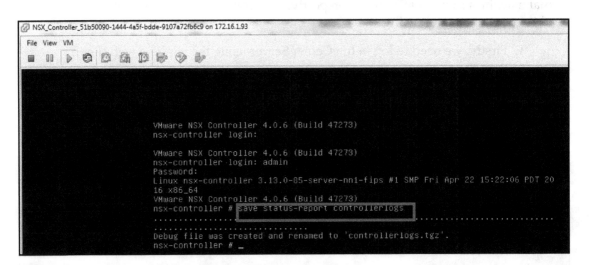

After the controller logs are captured, we can go ahead and copy the same set of logs to any machine that has got IP connectivity with the controller.

In the following example, I have copied the controller logs to one of the management ESXi host TMP locations:

```
nsx-controller # copy file controllerlogs.tgz root@172.16.1.93:/tmp
Password:
controllerlogs.tgz                         100%   142MB   47.2MB/s   00:03
nsx-controller # _
```

With that, we will move to NSX Edge and DLR log collection, and we will finish off with data plane log collection and a few important service statuses.

The processes for collecting Edge and DLR logs are almost the same.

Collecting Edge and Distributed Logical Router logs through the web client

The following are the steps for collecting distributed logical router logs:

1. Firstly, log into vCenter Server using the vSphere web client.
2. Click the **Networking & Security** icon.
3. Click **Edges** on the left-hand pane.
4. On the right-hand pane, select the edge (**DLR/EDGE**) we want to download from.
5. Click **Actions** and select **Download Tech support logs**.

In the following screenshot, we can see **Download Tech support log** highlighted for Distributed Logical Router, and I mentioned earlier that this is the same process as for collecting NSX Edge logs:

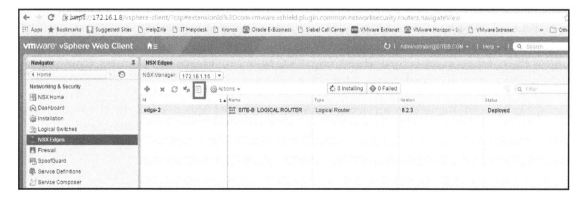

For collecting logs via CLI, we need to execute the following command by executing any of the following steps:

1. Using a vSphere client session, we can connect to vCenter Server or the ESXi host where controller is running, and we can take a VM console session to controller to leverage the CLI command for log collection.
2. Take an SSH session directly to controller and execute the CLI command for log collection:

```
export tech-support scp user@scpserver:file
```

We have already discussed what EAM is and the role it plays in an NSX environment. Apart from that vSphere troubleshooting piece, we need to the status and logging level of two user world agents, which will be running in an NSX-prepared ESXi host.

NSX user world agents

NSX Manager is responsible for deploying the NSX Controller cluster, ESXi hosts preparation by pushing **vSphere Installation Bundles** (**VIBs**) to enable VXLAN, distributed routing, distributed firewall, and a user world agent used to communicate at the control-plane level. The functionality of the user world agent is highly critical and any failures will have a direct impact on the control plane learning, which eventually affects data plane traffic. So, let's discuss these agents, along with basic health checks and log locations.

netcpa

It is a user world agent that communicates with NSX control plane, and the netcpa service should be up and running on the NSX-prepared ESXi host. If the functionality is impacted, we will certainly experience routing and switching issues in the NSX environment, and the ESXi host won't learn new routes from the time the netcpa service was down. So, this is extremely important: creating the routes alone on an NSX Edge VM won't do the trick; unless the netcpa service is up and running, ESXi host won't learn those routes. Complete the following steps in order to check for netcpa-related issues:

1. Check if the netcpa service is running on the host (this needs to be checked on the host where we are experiencing network or control-plane related issues).

2. Use the following command to check the netcpa service:

```
/etc/init.d/netcpad status
```

The following screenshot depicts the netcpa agent's status:

```
172.16.1.93 - PuTTY
[root@localhost:~] /etc/init.d/netcpad status
netCP agent service is running
[root@localhost:~]
```

Check if the netcpa configuration file is showing all the controllers. Use the following command to check controller details in the configuration file:

```
cat   /etc/vmare/netcpa/config-by-vsm.xml
```

The following screenshot depicts the config file output, with controller IP and SSL certificate thumbprint information:

```
[root@localhost:/etc/vmware/netcpa] cat config-by-vsm.xml
<config>
  <connectionList>
    <connection id="0000">
      <port>1234</port>
      <server>172.16.1.21</server>
      <sslEnabled>true</sslEnabled>
      <thumbprint>20:13:30:19:3A:B2:C5:87:B9:9C:C0:00:AB:98:B4:D5:BB:5B:5A:B5</thumbprint>
    </connection>
    <connection id="0001">
      <port>1234</port>
      <server>172.16.1.22</server>
      <sslEnabled>true</sslEnabled>
      <thumbprint>1F:A1:72:1B:D0:0E:E5:E6:21:46:AD:DC:9B:FF:C5:C6:53:EB:6D:0F</thumbprint>
    </connection>
    <connection id="0002">
      <port>1234</port>
      <server>172.16.1.23</server>
      <sslEnabled>true</sslEnabled>
      <thumbprint>33:6D:B7:E9:8B:1D:E5:58:EB:A5:D1:AC:81:69:2C:84:D4:8E:E4:33</thumbprint>
    </connection>
  </connectionList>
  <localeId>
    <id>564DDF7D-84CC-FC0D-6D34-3C38278531CA</id>
  </localeId>
```

In the `/var/log/netcpa.log` file on the ESXi host, we can see the complete netcpa logs. The following screenshot depicts controller registration information, which is populated in netcpa logs:

```
2016-07-20T08:20:57.963Z info netcpa[29081B70] [Originator@6876 sub=Default] Connected to vsfwd. Cookie id is 16
2016-07-20T08:20:58UTC rmqClient Server socket 16 hung up closing connection
2016-07-20T08:20:58.078Z info netcpa[FFA73B70] [Originator@6876 sub=Default] Got CLIENT CLOSE Message in CookieId 16
2016-07-20T08:21:28.080Z info netcpa[FFE40B70] [Originator@6876 sub=Default] host-id is host-63
2016-07-20T08:21:28.080Z info netcpa[FFE40B70] [Originator@6876 sub=Default] Connected to vsfwd. Cookie id is 16
2016-07-20T08:21:28.095Z info netcpa[FFA73B70] [Originator@6876 sub=Default] Received Registration ACK, can Start Sending Messages
2016-07-20T08:21:47.945Z info netcpa[FFA32B70] [Originator@6876 sub=Default] Received host credential message ...
2016-07-20T08:21:47.945Z info netcpa[FFA32B70] [Originator@6876 sub=Default] VSM configured privateKeyFile /etc/vmware/ssl/rui-for-netcpa.key, certi
sl/rui-for-netcpa.crt
2016-07-20T08:21:47.955Z info netcpa[FFA32B70] [Originator@6876 sub=Default] Received controller info message numConn 3 ...
2016-07-20T08:21:47.955Z info netcpa[FFA32B70] [Originator@6876 sub=Default] Added conn 172.16.1.21:1234::20:13:30:19:3A:B2:C5:87:B9:9C:C0:00:AB:98:
1 enabled(updated by VSM)
2016-07-20T08:21:47.955Z info netcpa[FFA32B70] [Originator@6876 sub=Default] Added conn 172.16.1.22:1234::1F:A1:72:1B:D0:0E:E5:E6:21:46:AD:DC:9B:FF:
1 enabled(updated by VSM)
2016-07-20T08:21:47.955Z info netcpa[FFA32B70] [Originator@6876 sub=Default] Added conn 172.16.1.23:1234::33:6D:B7:E9:8B:1D:E5:58:EB:A5:D1:AC:81:69:
1 enabled(updated by VSM)
2016-07-20T08:21:47.955Z info netcpa[FFA32B70] [Originator@6876 sub=Default] Core: Receive controller list(num 3) from ConfigManager
2016-07-20T08:21:47.955Z info netcpa[29081B70] [Originator@6876 sub=Default] App CORE : 0 register connection to new controller 172.16.1.23 port 123
2016-07-20T08:21:48.201Z info netcpa[FFA32B70] [Originator@6876 sub=Default] Received vdr dvs info message, number of entries 0 ...
2016-07-20T08:21:48.212Z info netcpa[FFA32B70] [Originator@6876 sub=Default] Received vdr instance message numVdrId 0 ...
```

Anytime we are facing issues with the netcpa service, I would strongly recommend restarting the service to confirm if that fixes the issue. To restart the netcpa service, we need to complete the following steps in order:

1. Log in as root to the ESXi host through SSH or through the DCUI console.
2. Run the `/etc/init.d/netcpad` restart command to restart the netcpa agent on the ESXi host.

Vsfwd

NSX distributed firewall is a hypervisor integrated firewall and apart from the point that the host should have a firewall `vib` installed, there should be a vsfwd daemon process up and running for proper message bus communication with NSX Manager.

The following command and screenshot shows a stateful firewall status on the ESXi host:

etc/init.d/vShield-Stateful-Firewall status

```
172.16.1.93 - PuTTY
[root@localhost:/etc/init.d]  /etc/init.d/vShield-Stateful-Firewall status
vShield-Stateful-Firewall is running
[root@localhost:/etc/init.d]
```

To check the active message bus session with NSX Manager the following command and screenshot depicts an active session with NSX Manager (172.16.1.5):

```
esxcli network ip connection list | grep 5671
```

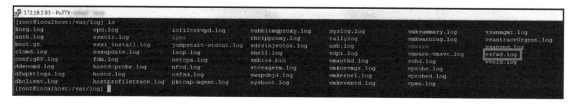

A potential failure can happen if port **5671** is not opened between the ESXi host and NSX Manager.

Vsfwd log location and collection process

NSX Distributed Firewall is a new generation firewall in vSphere environment used primarily because of its ability to filter traffic at the virtual machine NIC level. Hence, it is important to understand the log collection and a few troubleshooting steps related to this feature. So, let's get started.

Firstly, we need to start with the prerequisites to run **Distributed Firewall (DFW)**. There is no need for log collection, even if the following requirements are not met. The prerequisites for running DFW are as follows:

- VMware vCenter Server should be version 5.5 minimum
- VMware ESXi version should be at 5.1, 5.5, 6.0
- VMware NSX for vSphere 6.0 and later

All logs related to vsfwd will be at the following location, and their representation is shown in the figure:

```
/var/log/vsfwd.log file on the ESXi host
```

Collecting centralized logs from NSX Manager

Firstly, we need to log in to NSX Manager using the admin credentials and execute the following command:

```
export host-tech-support host-id scp uid@ip:/path
```

With the introduction of NSX 6.2.3, VMware has come up with an export host-tech-support command, which can be executed on the NSX Manager to collect the following information. I strongly believe they will be adding more and more log collection options, since this is a centralized way of collecting the logs, but a lot depends upon the type of failure. If we encounter an NSX Manager failure scenario, centralized logging functionality is also impacted, hence it is important to understand the next plan for such scenarios, which is the whole purpose of me explaining the log collection process so far. Following is the list of logs that are included in the centralized logs as of now:

- vmkernel and vsfwd log files
- A list of filters
- A list of dfw rules
- A list of containers
- Spoofguard details
- Host-related information
- ipdiscovery-related information
- RMQ command outputs
- Security group and services profile and instance details
- esxcli-related outputs

VXLAN troubleshooting

VXLAN is the overlay technology that is used in the VMware NSX environment when it comes to first-time testing and implementation, and most likely, we will end up with a few connectivity issues. Some of the common issues that we might face because of misconfiguration in both virtual and physical networks are as follows:

- Virtual machines have no network connectivity, either between other machines in the same VXLAN network, or no egress connection with the physical world

- Frequent packet drops getting reported and the applications team facing poor performance issues
- Virtual Machines have proper network connectivity on some of the ESXi hosts, but when placed on another set of hosts, there is no connectivity
- Normal ping tests are fine, but when checking with VXLAN packets, packet drops occur
- Virtual machines in VLAN networks have proper network connectivity; however, VXLAN networks are not working

The majority of network-related issues related to VXLAN will be around the preceding list of issues; however, only by applying our knowledge will we have a clear picture of what type of networks customers have and what type of network issues they are facing. So, let's get started with learning what the possible symptoms for such issues are and what the necessary actions to resolve the issue are.

After implementing a VXLAN solution, I would strongly recommend to checking GUI-level PING and VXLAN tests between all the NSX-prepared ESXi hosts, which is the best way to confirm if initial requirements are met for sending a VXLAN packet from one hypervisor to another hypervisor.

We need to select one of the logical switches. Go to **Monitor** page, and there we will have two options:

- **Ping**
- **Broadcast**

The following screenshot shows the **Ping** and **Broadcast** test options:

First, we will do a **Ping** test between the `172.16.1.94` and `172.16.1.96` ESXi hosts, and we will follow that with a VXLAN test. The following screenshot shows a successful Ping test:

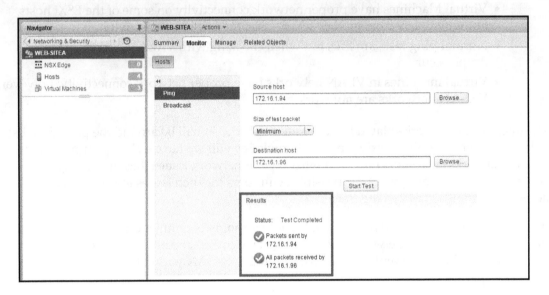

The following screenshot shows a VXLAN test between the same ESXi host, and we can confirm that VXLAN packets sent from host `172.16.1.94` are successfully accepted by `172.16.1.96`:

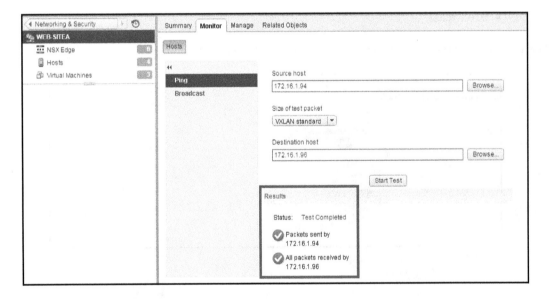

In addition to the previous test, we can also perform a VXLAN ping test through an SSH session, and I have captured the output of this test between two ESXi hosts. The command to perform the test is as follows:

```
ping ++netstack=vxlan -d -s MTU VTEP-IP
```

The following screenshot depicts a VXLAN test performed through an SSH session to host 172.16.1.94:

The preceding output is a clear indication that MTU is set properly in the VXLAN environment, so we are able to MTU more than 1500. If there is an MTU misconfiguration issue, this test would fail, as shown in the following screenshot. I intentionally changed MTU in the distributed virtual switch from 1600 to 1500 to showcase the failure scenario:

Network troubleshooting isn't complete without a packet capture. This is our final topic for this chapter, and I will showcase how to collect VXLAN packets. We will also take a quick walk-through to see what information is in the packet. Considering the knowledge we have gained so far, it should be a cakewalk for everyone.

Packet capturing and analysis

Starting from ESXi 5.5, the pktcap-uw tool is embedded inside the hypervisor. Some of you will be familiar with the tcpdump tool, which was already available in ESXi; pktcap is a replacement for the same. The prime reason for integrating the pktcap tool captures packets are every layer which is extremely essential in NSX world. So, we are no longer limited by capturing packets at the vmkernel layer. I have been a big fan of this tool starting from the vCloud networking and security days and I strongly believe most of us will like this tool. Before jumping into packet capturing, let's be clear about the following points:

- `Pktcap`, by default, collects only incoming packets, and it is unidirectional. So, if we want to capture both ingress and egress traffic, we need to add certain parameters. If not, the whole purpose of capturing the packet will be defeated.
- Traffic direction is mentioned as `-dir 0` for ingress packets.
- Traffic direction is mentioned as `-dir 1` for egress packets.
- We can capture a packet at the vmkernel, vmnic, and switch port levels (DVS).
- Detailed command syntax is available if we issue the following command in ESXi host:

```
Pktcap-uw -h
```

Enough theoryâ◎◎let's get started by capturing the packet to analyze the VXLAN field. Before that, let me explain my lab setup and virtual machine details so that we can verify if those outputs match the captured packet details.

Lab environment details

In this lab, I have two vSphere clusters, and we have a VXLAN network 5001, which is stretched across these two clusters. Both clusters have their own distributed switch.

The virtual machine IP in cluster A is `192.16.10.12`, with a VTEP IP of `172.16.1.32` running on ESXi `172.16.1.97`.

The virtual machine IP in cluster B is `192.16.10.14`, with a VTEP IP of `172.16.1.33` running on ESXi `172.16.1.94`.

VNIC packet capturing for egress traffic

To start the packet capturing, we need to take an SSH session to host `172.16.1.97` and identify on which VNIC the VM is running:

1. Issue the `ESXTOP` command and press the *n* key to show the network parameters. The following screenshot shows the ESXTOP screen. We have identified that our source virtual machine 192.16.10.12 is running on `vmnic0`:

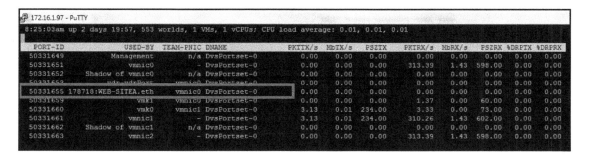

2. Issue the following command for egress traffic capturing. Output is saved in the ESXi host **tmp** directory:

```
pktcap-uw --uplink vmnic0 --dir 1 --stage 1 -o /tmp/webAvxlan.pcap
```

3. Initiate a `ping` request from the source virtual machine to the destination virtual machine, as shown in the following screenshot:

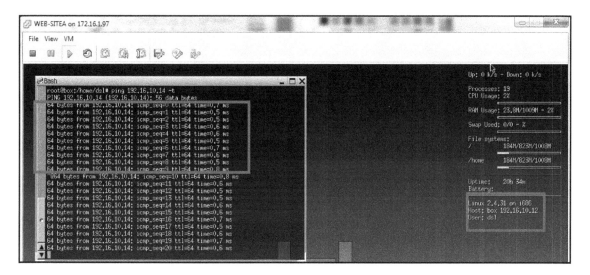

4. Stop the packet capture after some time by pressing *Ctrl + C* in an ESXi putty session and see the following output:

```
172.16.1.97 - PuTTY
[root@localhost:~] pktcap-uw --uplink vmnic0 --dir 1 --stage 1 -o /tmp/webAvxlan.pcap
The name of the uplink is vmnic0
The dir is Tx
The Stage is Post
The output file is /tmp/webAvxlan.pcap
No server port specifed, select 43322 as the port
Local CID 2
Listen on port 43322
Accept...Vsock connection from port 1534 cid 2
Dump: 21, broken : 0, drop: 0, file err: 0Join with dump thread failedDestroying session 2

Dumped 21 packet to file /tmp/webAvxlan.pcap, dropped 0 packets.
Done.
[root@localhost:~]
```

5. The saved packet webAvxlan.pcap needs to be imported to the Wireshark tool. I know for sure that everyone knows how to copy or download a file from the ESXi host.

6. Once we import the file to Wireshark, we will get the following output:

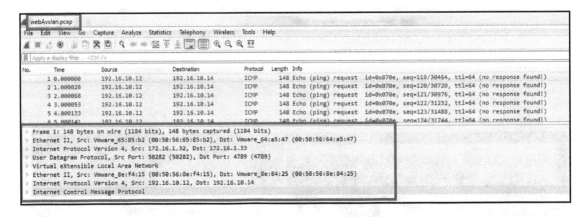

7. Expand the **Virtual eXentsible Local Area Network** option, which will display the complete VXLAN header field as shown in the following screenshot:

```
▷ Frame 1: 148 bytes on wire (1184 bits), 148 bytes captured (1184 bits)
▷ Ethernet II, Src: Vmware_65:85:b2 (00:50:56:65:85:b2), Dst: Vmware_64:a5:47 (00:50:56:64:a5:47)
▷ Internet Protocol Version 4, Src: 172.16.1.32, Dst: 172.16.1.33    Outer IP Field
▷ User Datagram Protocol, Src Port: 50282 (50282), Dst Port: 4789 (4789)    VXLAN UDP PORT
▲ Virtual eXtensible Local Area Network
   ▲ Flags: 0x0800, VXLAN Network ID (VNI)
        0... .... .... .... = GBP Extension: Not defined
        .... .... .0.. .... = Don't Learn: False
        .... 1... .... .... = VXLAN Network ID (VNI): True
        .... .... .... 0... = Policy Applied: False
        .000 .000 0.00 .000 = Reserved(R): False
     Group Policy ID: 0
     VXLAN Network Identifier (VNI): 5001    VXLAN ID(Segment-ID)
     Reserved: 0
▷ Ethernet II, Src: Vmware_8e:f4:15 (00:50:56:8e:f4:15), Dst: Vmware_8e:84:25 (00:50:56:8e:84:25)
▷ Internet Protocol Version 4, Src: 192.16.10.12, Dst: 192.16.10.14    Inner IP Field
▷ Internet Control Message Protocol
```

As we can see from the highlighted field, we got the following output, which matches perfectly with the lab environment details that we mentioned earlier:

- The inner IP Src is 192.16.10.12 and Dst is 192.16.10.14 (two machines which we have tested the ping command)
- The VXLAN network is 5001 (the logical switch where our virtual machines are running)
- The VXLAN UDP port is 4789
- The outer IP SRC: 172.16.1.32 and DST: 172.16.1.33 (VXLAN tunnel endpoint IP address)

I strongly believe this is the most precise VXLAN output, which will help us in many scenarios, and pktcap-uw is a great tool, which is not used by many people, primarily because of lack of knowledge. With the captured output imported to the **Wireshark** tool, it gives us granular-level information on all the fields. So, keep these steps handy and I bet this will be useful in a production environment.

NSX upgrade checklist and planning order

It is always better to stop something from happening in the first instance than spend time repairing the damage after it has happened. Every product upgrade should follow a step-by-step process with proper planning, and an NSX upgrade is no exception. The following steps are the proper order that needs to be followed while planning to upgrade the NSX environment:

1. Upgrade NSX Manager
2. Upgrade NSX Controllers
3. Upgrade ESXi cluster prepared by NSX
4. Upgrade Distributed Logical Router and Edge service gateway
5. Upgrade data security and guest introspection services

First and foremost, we need to ensure the following pre-checks are met before doing any upgrade.

The following is an NSX pre-upgrade checklist:

- Take backup for NSX Manager. In a cross-VC NSX environment, we need to take backup from all the NSX Managers and complete the following process for all NSX Managers.
- Take a snapshot of all NSX Managers. This is only for additional protection in case normal backups are not available or corrupted due to human error or catastrophic events.
- Log in to NSX Manager and run show filesystems to show the /dev/sda2 filesystem usage. If the filesystem usage is 100 percent, the upgrade process will certainly fail, and for such cases, we need to purge manager logs and NSX system commands and reboot the NSX Manager before starting with the upgrade.
- Issue the following commands in NSX Manager to purge NSX logs and system commands:
  - purge log manager
  - purge log system
- Reboot the NSX Manager appliance for the log cleanup to take effect.
- NSX data security should be uninstalled before upgrading NSX Manager.
- Ensure all controllers are connected and don't plan to deploy any new controllers during the existing controller upgrade phase.

- Place the vSphere cluster ESXi host in maintenance mode, perform the upgrade, and reboot the host. Continue the same operation for the NSX-prepared ESXi host, so that new VIBS are pushed to all ESXi hosts, and finally, take the host out of maintenance mode.
- Starting from NSX Manager 6.2.3 onwards the default VXLAN port is 4789. Before NSX 6.2.3, the default VXLAN UDP port number was 8472. So, if we are planning to continue with the new VXLAN port 4789, please ensure that this port is allowed in your firewall.
- NSX Edge and NSX Distributed Logical Router control VM can be upgraded in any order, and there is no repeated upgrade process for HA-enabled NSX Edge and control VM. Both appliances get upgraded at the same time.
- Finally, we can go ahead and upgrade the guest introspection virtual machine and respective partner appliance.
- Once the upgrade is complete, we should delete all snapshots taken for NSX Manager, after verifying all components and services are up and running.

The following screenshot depicts all operationally-impacted tasks, and non-impacted tasks and services during respective NSX component upgrade phases:

NSX Components	Operational impact	Not impacted
NSX Manager	NSX Manager GUI and API-related new tasks are blocked	Control plane and data plane continue to work
NSX Controllers	No modification accepted for logical networks and no new logical network creation will be accepted	Management plane and data plane
vSphere Cluster	No new VM provisioning will be accepted during this phase for that specific vSphere cluster.	Management plane, control plane, and data plane related tasks for other vSphere clusters will be working (if we are doing upgrades on one vSphere cluster at a time)
NSX Edge and Control VM	All Edge and control VM services will be impacted during this operation.	Management plane, new Edges and control VM can be deployed. All existing configuration on old edges will be retained.
Guest introspection and data security	Virtual machines will be unprotected during this phase	All other NSX related tasks and services will be intact.

That concludes our final chapter, and I believe this network virtualization journey has been fantastic so far.

The future of NSX

The current and future choice of IT will certainly be Software Defined Data Center, no doubt about it. One of the primary reasons I believe this product and technology is the cherry on top of the VMware product portfolio is the proven and larger ecosystem that VMware has, and the fact that customers can leverage NSX in private, public (vCloud Air), and with the mix of both, a truly hybrid cloud platform. There are millions of workloads, which are protected by vCloud Air disaster recovery data center, and behind the scenes, these are vSphere environments that are fully network-virtualized with NSX. It's no mistake that Gartner has recently recognized the vCloud Air disaster recovery solution as one of the best in the public Cloud market. The VMware NSX approach is very simple: *Follow the virtual machines wherever they go: private, public, or hybrid will always remain secured*. From a cross-vendor perspective, there are definitely some hard decisions taken by VMware, especially with products such as NEXUS 1000V, which is no longer supported with VMware NSX. However, in a greenfield deployment scenario, there is only one question that might be raised while looking for an NSX solution: what is the cost and manpower involved in developing or remodeling existing applications if NSX is getting integrated? Does it demand an overall change in networking? Does it demand any specific models of switches or routers? We all have the answers now: NSX doesn't demand any significant change in overall physical networking. Already a recognized leader in software defined networking, VMware has made another wise move by acquiring Arkin on June 13, 2016, and that will further simplify a lot of NSX operational tasks. Arkin cross-domain visibility will help customers to get a granular visibility on physical to overlay mapping and other security parameters, and with that approach and output, day-to-day operational tasks will be much more simplified. How many times have we received questions about how a virtual machine is connected to the network? The traditional way of checking that would be by taking multiple connections to multiple products to get an end-to-end connectivity view. I strongly believe tasks like this will be simplified with the integration of Arkin with NSX, and adding to that, it will give us precise information on what types of traffic we have in the data center, as well as overall traffic percentages for East-West and North-South, Internet traffic, as a few examples.

VMware vRealize network insight (Arkin) is an intelligent security and operations management solution for the network, which provides 360-degree visibility across virtual and physical networks using network flow analytics. It is available for download from 1st August 2016. There was also a recent announcement from VMware regarding a new release of NSX multi hypervisor called NSX transformers, which supports hypervisors such as KVM and vSphere, and one could simply club them under a common NSX transport zone. It's too early to comment on how transformers will evolve, so for the time being, it will be a watch and wait game for all of us. NSX is certainly an evolution in software-defined networking, and it has got all the bits and fragments needed to reach further heights, which will enormously help all types of businesses. I appreciate you all being part of this journey and I would encourage everyone to start testing and implementing this great solution. Let's be part of this game-changing software. Based on your technical background and the pace at which we can understand and learn a technology, I believe there will be a few questions, and I would appreciate if you all can reach out to me via LinkedIn. Rest assured I will ensure queries are addressed at the earliest opportunity.

Summary

We started this chapter with Introduction to troubleshooting followed by NSX manager,Controller and Data plane log collection and major focus points when things go wrong. Finally we ended this chapter with Future of NSX followed by few links for documentation reading.

References

Lastly, as promised earlier, I'm posting all the articles that we all should read. You can trust me that the right way to climb the NSX ladder is by reading each and every document available; it will only multiply our knowledge:

- The CISCO NEXUS 9000 design guide, which talks about a few design scenarios with UCS servers. A great guide for physical network design understanding with NSX: `http://www.vmware.com/content/dam/digitalmarketing/vmware/en/pdf/whitepaper/products/nsx/design-guide-for-nsx-with-cisco-nexus-9-and-ucs-white-paper.pdf`
- Advanced networking services offered through vCloud Air. It is worth reading this document to know how NSX is helping vCloud Air customers and what services are offered by providing zero trust security in the public Cloud: `http://vcloud.vmware.com/service-offering/advanced-networking-services`

- The VMware NSX design guide for vSphere is another knowledge hub for designing NSX in a vSphere environment: `http://www.vmware.com/content/da m/digitalmarketing/vmware/en/pdf/products/nsx/vmw-nsx-network-virtua lization-design-guide.pdf`

- We should all go through this blog if we really want to keep ourselves updated with the technology. This is a network virtualization blog from VMware, and there is good amount of videos and use cases discussed: `http://blogs.vmware.c om/networkvirtualization/#.V5NUP195QI`

- VMware integrated OpenStack with NSX configuration guide. This document demands a little bit of VIO knowledge; however, readers will find out how NSX works in the VIO world: `https://communities.vmware.com/docs/DOC-3985`

- The complete guide to upgrading VCNS to NSX. This guide contains step-by-step instructions to upgrade all vCloud network security solutions to NSX: `https://p ubs.vmware.com/NSX-62/topic/com.vmware.ICbase/PDF/nsx_62_upgrade.pdf`

- I'm going to shout practice, practice, practice! Well, practice makes perfect, so keep practicing the free VMware HOL labs. I would highly recommend starting with vSphere distributed switch from A to Z labs before starting NSX labs: `http: //labs.hol.vmware.com/HOL/catalogs/catalog/13`

- The document is a deployment guide for implementing VMware NSX with Brocade VCS: `http://www.brocade.com/content/html/en/deployment-guide/ brocade-vcs-gateway-vmware-dp/GUID-329954A2-A957-4864-AE-FD29262D33 52.html`

Index

www.ingramcontent.com/pod-product-compliance
Lightning Source LLC
Chambersburg PA
CBHW060531060326
40690CB00017B/3448